Show Up More Relationally

A Simple Guide to Reconnecting With Others Without Losing Yourself.

Jim Sabellico

ONE

Alone in a Room Full of People

If you've ever walked into a room full of people and still felt alone, you're not broken. You're human.

It's strange, isn't it? You can have friends, a partner, a family, a full calendar and still feel unseen. Still feel like no one really gets you. Still feel like you're performing the role of connection instead of actually living it.

I know that feeling. I've been surrounded and starving at the same time. Showing up for everyone else but somehow disappearing in the process. It's a kind of loneliness that doesn't come from isolation. It comes from disconnection from yourself, from others, or both.

And that's really what this book is about.

Not fixing people. Not teaching you how to "communicate better" or "win arguments." It's about **relearning how to show up**. For yourself first, and then for the people who matter most.

Because here's the truth: the quality of your relationships will always mirror the quality of your relationship with yourself. If you ignore your needs, you'll end up expecting others to meet them. If you silence your voice, you'll attract people who are comfortable not hearing it. If you keep performing to be liked, you'll eventually forget what real love feels like.

Showing up relationally doesn't start with anyone else. It starts with you.

It starts with slowing down enough to notice the patterns that keep repeating. The exhaustion, the resentment, the way you say "it's fine" when it's clearly not. It starts with asking better questions instead of giving faster answers. It starts with the courage to be honest, even when honesty changes things.

This isn't a how-to manual. It's a companion. I'm not here to tell you what you're doing wrong. I'm here to walk beside you as you uncover what's been missing. The parts of connection that feel real, grounded, and safe.

We'll talk about the traps that keep people stuck: people-pleasing, losing yourself in love, using relationships like currency, and holding on long after something's over. We'll talk about boundaries, honesty, friendship, and the hard work of letting go without bitterness. But mostly, we'll talk about learning to be present, with yourself and with others, in a way that finally feels like peace.

If you're tired of performing, of fixing, of trying to make every relationship "work" while slowly running out of yourself, take a breath. You don't have to earn connection. You just have to show up for it honestly, imperfectly, consistently.

That's what this journey is. Not about having more people around you, but about being more *you* around the people you already have.

So wherever you are rebuilding, grieving, searching, or just trying to understand why you feel disconnected, you're in the right place.

We'll take it one step at a time, together.

Let's learn what it really means to show up more relationally.

TWO

Relationship Number One

When most people think about relationships, they think about the ones that connect them to others. They think about the people they love, the friends they trust, or the coworkers they depend on. Rarely does anyone stop to consider the one relationship that shapes all the rest: the one they have with themselves.

It sounds simple, but the truth is that how you relate to yourself determines the quality of every other connection in your life. If you're impatient with yourself, that impatience will bleed into the way you speak to others. If you don't believe your needs matter, you'll naturally attract people who agree with that belief. If you spend your life overextending to be liked, you'll never really know what love without performance feels like. Every external relationship is a mirror of your internal one, whether you notice it or not.

For years, I didn't see it that way. I thought being selfless was the same as being loving. I thought that showing up for everyone else meant I was doing the right thing. The problem was that I was showing up for everyone except me. I could take care of anyone, manage any crisis, hold any burden. I was dependable, steady, and strong. But underneath all of that, I was quietly exhausted. I had become so used to meeting everyone else's needs that I had lost touch with my own. What I called "being strong" was actually a way of hiding how disconnected I had become from myself.

That's the trap many of us fall into. We spend so much energy trying to be good partners, parents, and friends that we forget to be good to ourselves. We treat self-respect like a reward instead of a responsibility. We think rest is something we earn only after everyone else is taken care of. But the truth is, neglecting yourself in the name of love eventually destroys the very love you're trying to preserve. You can only give what you have. If all you have left is depletion, that's what ends up spilling out.

Learning to show up for yourself doesn't mean becoming selfish or distant. It means learning to be honest about what's happening inside you. It means paying attention to your signals instead of pushing through them. It means noticing when you're tired and allowing yourself to rest without guilt. It means saying no when your capacity is gone, even if saying yes would make someone else more comfortable. It's about creating enough internal safety that you no longer rely on others to make you feel seen, valued, or at peace.

That kind of honesty can feel strange at first. When you've built your identity around taking care of everyone else, turning that care inward can feel unnatural. You may even feel guilty for it. But caring for yourself is not betrayal. It's stewardship. It's taking responsibility for your own energy, your own peace, and your own emotional balance. No one else can do that for you, no matter how much they love you.

Start small. It might mean keeping a promise to yourself that no one else will ever see. It might mean making space for quiet in the middle of a noisy day. It might mean allowing yourself to admit that something isn't working and that you don't have to keep pretending that it is. Over time, those small acts begin to rebuild the trust between you and you. And that trust becomes the foundation of every other relationship you'll ever have.

Because once you start showing up for yourself with honesty and compassion, something shifts. You stop chasing connection from a place of emptiness and start creating it from a place of fullness. You stop needing people to complete you and start inviting them to complement you. You stop viewing love as something to earn and begin to experience it as something to share.

Every relationship in your life will change when this one does. The healthier your relationship with yourself becomes, the more naturally you'll recognize what feels right and what doesn't. You'll stop overexplaining. You'll stop apologizing for existing. You'll stop giving people the parts of you that are meant to rest. And as you do, you'll notice that connection starts to feel easier. You'll still give, but not from fear. You'll still love, but not from lack.

That's what it means to show up relationally. Not to become someone else's source of peace, but to bring peace into the room because you've already cultivated it within yourself. It starts here, with you. Always with you.

THREE

The Mirror Principle

There was a person in my life who used to frustrate me endlessly. Every conversation turned into a competition. No matter what I said, they had to one-up it. If I shared something meaningful, they'd find a way to make it about them. I'd walk away angry, wondering how someone could be so blind to their own arrogance.

At first, I told myself they were just difficult. I started avoiding their calls, limiting my time around them, and venting to others about how exhausting they were. But even with distance, I noticed something that bothered me more than their behavior. The same frustration followed me into other relationships. Different faces, same feeling. That's when it hit me.

It wasn't just about them.

What I was really angry about wasn't their need to dominate the conversation. It was how easily I gave up my place in it. I didn't stand firm when they interrupted. I didn't protect my voice when they dismissed it. I stayed quiet, stewing in silence, convincing myself I was taking the high road when really, I was avoiding my own discomfort.

The mirror was clear. It wasn't showing me their flaws. It was showing me mine.

That realization changed everything. I started paying closer attention to the people who triggered me most. Every time someone brought up strong emotion — anger, irritation, defensiveness, guilt — I began asking myself what part of me they were reflecting. The answers were uncomfortable but honest.

The friend who constantly complained reminded me of the version of me that used to need rescuing. The person who talked over me mirrored the part of me that still doubted whether my thoughts mattered. The family member who judged me was holding up a reflection of the inner critic I had carried for years.

Every person became a mirror, reflecting something within me that needed to be seen.

It wasn't about blame. It was about awareness.

The mirror principle teaches that what you notice most strongly in others — whether positive or negative — often reveals what is active within you. The qualities you admire in others are the ones you're ready to grow into. The traits that frustrate you are often the ones you haven't fully resolved in yourself. It's not about agreeing with bad behavior or excusing hurtful actions. It's about taking the opportunity to look inward before you react outward.

Once you understand that, every interaction becomes a teacher.

At first, this awareness can sting. You might realize that many of your frustrations have less to do with what others are doing and more to do with how you feel when they do it. Someone interrupts you, and it touches the part of you that has felt invisible for years. Someone rejects you, and it triggers the part that still doubts your worth. Someone gets distant, and it awakens old fear that love will always leave. These reactions don't make you weak. They make you human. The mirror isn't meant to shame you. It's meant to free you from repeating what you don't even realize you're repeating.

The challenge is that the mirror doesn't always tell you what you want to hear. Sometimes it exposes a truth you've been avoiding. Maybe you're more controlling than you want to admit. Maybe your kindness is sometimes a disguise for fear. Maybe the pattern you keep blaming others for is one you're quietly maintaining. The first instinct is usually to look away, to focus on how wrong the other person is. But that's how cycles stay alive. You can't change what you won't acknowledge.

When you start using the mirror consciously, relationships become a path of growth rather than a battlefield. You begin to notice your patterns with compassion instead of judgment. You stop seeing yourself as a victim of people's behavior and start seeing yourself as an active participant in every interaction. You begin to ask better questions. What is this moment trying to teach me about me? What part of me feels threatened right now? What old story am I reliving through this situation?

That kind of awareness takes practice, but over time, it changes everything.

There's a man I once worked with who had an uncanny ability to stay calm in chaos. I admired it, but it also bothered me. His calmness felt like dismissal. When things got tense, I wanted a reaction. I wanted urgency. Instead, he stayed grounded, almost unshakable. At first, I saw it as arrogance. But the more I reflected, the more I realized that what I was labeling as arrogance was actually confidence — something I hadn't yet cultivated in myself. My discomfort wasn't about his stillness. It was about my lack of it. Once I saw that, my irritation disappeared. I began to appreciate his steadiness instead of resenting it.

That's how the mirror works both ways. It shows you not only what's unhealed but also what's possible. The people who inspire you are mirrors too. They reflect the potential you already carry. When you admire someone's honesty, it's because there's a part of you longing to live that openly. When you respect someone's strength, it's because you know that same resilience is already in you, waiting to be developed.

The mirror becomes dangerous only when you don't realize it's there. If you look at every relationship and assume it's all about the other person, you stay powerless. You keep reliving the same patterns with new faces. You keep asking, "Why do I attract people like this?" instead of asking, "What in me keeps responding this way?" The mirror turns chaos into clarity once you stop avoiding it.

This doesn't mean every conflict is your fault. Sometimes people are unkind or unfair, and that's on them. But even in those moments, the mirror still offers you insight. It might be showing you where you need to set firmer boundaries. It might be reminding you that you deserve better. It might be teaching you that you're capable of walking away without bitterness. There's always something to learn.

The mirror principle doesn't just apply to pain. It also shows up in joy. The friend who makes you feel safe is showing you how far you've come in learning to trust. The partner who loves you well reflects the self-worth you've cultivated. The relationships that feel peaceful are proof of your growth. The mirror keeps working, even when life feels calm.

Understanding this truth transforms how you show up in the world. Instead of being reactive, you become reflective. Instead of blaming others, you become curious. Instead of repeating old stories, you begin to write new ones.

Every time you feel triggered or moved by someone, imagine holding up a mirror and asking, "What is this showing me?" At first, the answers might surprise you. Over time, they will liberate you.

You'll notice that life keeps handing you the same kind of situation until you respond differently. The friend who takes advantage of your kindness. The partner who avoids emotional depth. The coworker who always undermines you. It's not punishment. It's repetition with purpose. The universe keeps handing you the same mirror until you finally see what it's trying to show you.

When you do, something shifts. The lesson stops repeating. The reflection changes. The same type of people stop showing up because you've stopped needing them to teach the same thing.

That's the quiet power of self-awareness. When you see yourself clearly, you attract differently. You respond differently. You love differently.

So the next time someone frustrates you, take a moment before reacting. Breathe. Instead of rushing to defend or explain, ask yourself what part of you feels exposed. If someone's words make you angry, what truth might they have touched? If someone's silence feels unbearable, what fear is it bringing to the surface? Awareness turns every trigger into a teacher.

And when you begin to see others through that lens, compassion grows naturally. You start to understand that everyone is doing the best they can with what they know, just like you. You start to realize that even when people act carelessly, they're often acting from their own pain. That doesn't make it acceptable, but it does make it understandable.

When you practice the mirror principle long enough, peace replaces defensiveness. You no longer need to win every argument. You don't have to prove your point to feel seen. You stop expecting people to behave a certain way because you understand that their actions are their reflection, not yours.

That kind of freedom changes the quality of every relationship. You can stand firm without being rigid, honest without being harsh, compassionate without being naïve. You can stay grounded even when others are chaotic.

The mirror principle teaches you to meet life with both accountability and grace. You learn to own your part, release what isn't yours, and move through the world with clarity instead of confusion.

It's not about becoming perfect. It's about becoming aware. The mirror doesn't judge you. It simply shows you where you are so you can decide who you want to become next.

So when someone frustrates you, instead of asking, "What's wrong with them?" start asking, "What is this showing me about me?" That single shift can change your relationships, your peace, and your life.

Because the truth is, the mirror never lies. It only waits for you to look.

FOUR

The People-Pleasing Trap

For most of my life, I believed being liked was the same thing as being kind. I thought that if I could keep everyone around me happy, I'd be safe, loved, and accepted. It sounds noble on the surface, who doesn't want to be the person everyone can count on? But underneath it, people-pleasing isn't about kindness. It's about fear.

I learned this lesson sitting across from someone I cared deeply about, trying to smooth over an argument that wasn't mine to fix. I apologized for things I didn't do, said "it's fine" when it wasn't, and smiled through words that were breaking me inside. The whole time, I felt my chest tightening, like my body knew what my mouth wouldn't admit.

When the conversation ended, they were calm again. But I wasn't. I left that room realizing something that changed me forever. I hadn't been trying to make peace. I'd been trying to avoid rejection.

That's the hidden root of people-pleasing. It's not selflessness. It's survival. Somewhere along the way, you learned that love is conditional, that it can be taken away if you disappoint someone. So you shape-shift. You adapt. You anticipate needs before they're spoken, manage emotions that aren't yours, and make yourself smaller so no one gets upset. It looks generous, but it's a quiet form of self-abandonment.

People-pleasing feels safe because it's familiar. It gives the illusion of control. If you can just keep everyone happy, you think maybe you'll finally feel at peace. But that peace never comes. Because every time you trade your truth for approval, a little part of you disappears.

You tell yourself it's not a big deal. That it's easier to let things go than to start a fight. That you're being "the bigger person." But eventually, you start to notice the cost. The exhaustion. The resentment. The subtle bitterness that builds when you realize no one's noticing your sacrifices because you've trained them not to.

At first, people-pleasing looks like compassion. Over time, it turns into quiet anger. You give and give, and eventually you start to feel invisible. The very strategy you used to stay connected becomes the reason you feel so disconnected.

I once worked with a woman who seemed to carry everyone's problems like they were her own. She was always the first to volunteer, the first to listen, the first to show up. But when she talked about her own needs, her voice would fade. One day, she told me something that stuck with me. "I'm afraid that if I ever stop taking care of everyone, they'll realize I was never worth keeping." That sentence broke my heart because I knew exactly what it felt like to believe that.

That's the lie at the center of people-pleasing, the belief that your worth depends on your usefulness. It's a belief that starts young, often in families or environments where love had strings attached. Maybe you learned to read the room before you could read words. Maybe you became the peacekeeper in a chaotic home. Maybe you were praised for being "easy," "helpful," or "good," and those words became the foundation of your identity. So as an adult, you keep earning connection the only way you know how, by serving, fixing, or sacrificing.

But healthy relationships don't require you to disappear to be loved.

When you live to please, you train people to expect your silence. You become the steady one, the caretaker, the rock. People come to you when they need something but rarely ask how you're doing. It's not because they don't care. It's because they've learned, through repetition, that you'll take care of yourself last.

And so the cycle continues. You please. They expect. You grow resentful. Then you feel guilty for being resentful. That guilt drives you to please again. It's an exhausting loop that keeps you emotionally stuck.

Breaking it starts with honesty. Not with other people, but with yourself. You have to admit that some of the "nice things" you do aren't really about love, they're about fear. Fear of conflict. Fear of being disliked. Fear of being alone. When you start telling yourself the truth about that, you reclaim the power you've been giving away.

When you stop trying to manage everyone else's comfort, you start to notice how uncomfortable you've become in your own life. You realize how often you say yes when your body screams no. You notice how hard it is to let someone else be disappointed in you, even for a moment. You start to see how much of your identity has been built on keeping the peace instead of living in truth.

But here's the beauty of that awareness, it's the first step back to freedom.

When you start practicing honesty, the people who truly love you won't run. They'll adjust. They might be surprised at first, but they'll learn that your "no" isn't rejection. It's respect. The people who only valued you for what you gave them might fall away, and that will hurt. But that pain is cleansing. It makes room for real connection.

You'll start to notice that not every disagreement is dangerous. You'll learn that conflict can actually deepen trust when handled with truth. You'll see that being liked is not the same thing as being loved.

And slowly, you'll begin to find peace that doesn't depend on other people's moods.

The process takes time. People-pleasing isn't just a habit — it's a nervous system pattern. You've spent years training your body to equate harmony with safety. So when you start speaking up, it feels like danger. Your pulse quickens, your chest tightens, and part of you wants to retreat. That's normal. It's your body learning that honesty isn't a threat. You're re-teaching yourself that your voice won't destroy love.

The next time you feel that urge to smooth things over, pause. Notice what's happening underneath. Are you doing this out of love or out of fear? Are you helping or rescuing? Are you showing kindness or performing it to stay liked?

If the answer feels uncomfortable, that's where your work begins.

Start with small, honest moments. Say "I can't take that on right now" without apologizing. Tell someone, "That comment hurt." Let a friend be upset with you and resist the urge to fix it. Each time you choose truth over approval, your self-respect grows. And as your self-respect grows, your relationships begin to shift.

Healthy people won't punish you for having boundaries. They'll appreciate you for being real. The wrong ones will fall away, but they were never meant to stay.

The greatest misunderstanding about people-pleasing is that it makes you loving. It doesn't. It makes you available. There's a difference. Love rooted in fear isn't love, it's survival. Real love requires honesty. It requires two people who can meet as equals, not one who keeps disappearing to hold the peace.

The moment you stop chasing approval, you open the door for authenticity. And when you live that way, the right people find you. The ones who value your honesty, not your compliance. The ones who don't need you to shrink for them to feel safe.

You don't have to stop caring. You just have to stop carrying what isn't yours. You don't have to become hard or distant to protect yourself. You just have to stop confusing peacekeeping with love.

When you finally release the need to please, something amazing happens. You start showing up as yourself. Fully. Clearly. Honestly. And that version of you, the one that's no longer performing, pretending, or walking on eggshells, becomes magnetic.

Because authenticity doesn't just attract love. It sustains it.

FIVE

The Cost of Keeping the Peace

For most of your life, you've probably been told that keeping the peace is a good thing. Walk away. Don't argue. Let it go. Be the bigger person. And sometimes, that advice makes sense. Not every disagreement is worth a battle. But when "keeping the peace" becomes your default setting, it stops being peaceful. It becomes a quiet form of self-betrayal.

There is a big difference between peacekeeping and peacemaking. Peacekeeping means staying silent to avoid conflict. Peacemaking means facing conflict honestly to create understanding. One preserves appearances. The other builds truth. One keeps everyone calm on the surface. The other invites everyone to grow beneath it.

The danger of constant peacekeeping is that it teaches you to disconnect from your own voice. You start measuring your words not by truth but by how little they will upset others. You learn to smooth things over even when they feel wrong. You convince yourself that silence is maturity when it's really fear in disguise. Over time, you become so practiced at avoiding conflict that you can't even tell the difference between peace and suppression.

I lived a lot of my life this way. I told myself that I was being wise by not stirring the pot. I believed that as long as things looked calm, they were healthy. But calm and healthy are not the same thing. You can have quiet in a room full of resentment. You can have smiles in a relationship full of avoidance. And you can have "peace" that costs you your voice, your truth, and eventually, your connection.

What I didn't realize back then was that every time I chose silence over honesty, I was slowly training people to believe that my comfort didn't matter. I was teaching them that I would always yield, always adjust, always carry the tension for everyone else. I thought I was protecting relationships, but I was really protecting dysfunction. The version of peace I was fighting for wasn't peace at all. It was control. I wanted everyone to be okay so that I could finally feel okay.

The irony is that when you avoid conflict long enough, it always finds you anyway. The truth has a way of waiting until it can no longer be ignored. The feelings you bury don't disappear. They ferment. They show up later as bitterness, sarcasm, and exhaustion. They show up as emotional distance. They show up as the moment you finally snap over something

small because you've spent years pretending the big things
didn't matter.

Real peace requires confrontation. Not with hostility, but with
honesty. It asks you to speak when silence becomes deception.
It asks you to tell the truth even when it shakes the illusion
that everything is fine. It doesn't mean you have to fight. It
means you have to stop hiding.

Learning to practice peacemaking instead of peacekeeping
takes courage. It means you will have to let go of being seen
as agreeable. It means you will have to accept that not
everyone will like your honesty. It means you will sometimes
have to sit in discomfort while the truth settles. But it also
means you will start to trust yourself again.

When you stop peacekeeping, you start creating space for real
relationship. People finally know where they stand with you.
You no longer build resentment under the surface because
your boundaries are clear. You can disagree without
disconnecting. You can speak your mind without losing your
calm. You can stay in conversation even when it gets messy,
because you know that truth and love are not opposites.
They're partners.

If you've spent years being the peacekeeper, this shift will feel
strange at first. You may find yourself worrying that you've
become harsh or selfish. You might see people pull back
because they were used to the version of you that absorbed all
the tension for them. That's okay. It's not your job to protect
everyone from discomfort. It's your job to bring honesty into
the room and let others decide what to do with it.

Healthy relationships can handle hard truths. Unhealthy ones depend on you never telling them. The moment you start telling the truth, the balance changes. The people who value authenticity will move closer. The ones who value control will move away. That's not loss. That's clarity.

So the next time you feel tempted to keep the peace, pause and ask yourself what that peace will cost. If your silence requires you to betray what you know is right, it's not peace. It's avoidance. If your quiet is fueled by fear, it's not strength. It's survival.

True peace is not the absence of tension. It's the presence of honesty. It's being able to look at someone you love and say, "This matters to me. I'm not here to argue. I'm here to be real." That's what builds lasting connection. Not pretending, not performing, not walking on eggshells.

The cost of keeping the peace is always authenticity. And once you've experienced real connection built on truth, you'll never want to pay that price again.

SIX

Losing Yourself in Love

Love can be one of the most beautiful experiences in life, but it can also be one of the most confusing. It starts out feeling like connection, partnership, and purpose. You meet someone who makes you feel seen in ways you haven't felt before. The world feels a little brighter, a little safer. You start adjusting to fit them, not because they asked you to, but because it feels good to belong somewhere. At first, it seems harmless. But over time, if you're not careful, belonging can slowly turn into becoming.

Many people lose themselves in love without realizing it. They merge so deeply into another person's world that they forget they had one of their own. Their opinions soften to match. Their routines shift. Their preferences blur. They call it compromise, but what's really happening is quiet erasure. You start to disappear one small decision at a time. It doesn't happen dramatically. It happens gradually, so slowly that by the time you notice it, you're not sure how to find your way back.

When your sense of identity fuses with a relationship, you begin to define yourself by it. You start seeing yourself through the lens of how the other person feels about you. If they're happy, you're enough. If they're distant, you're not. If they're proud of you, you feel valuable. If they're disappointed, you feel small. Your emotional state becomes tethered to their approval. Without realizing it, you hand over the power to decide who you are.

That kind of fusion might feel like love, but it isn't. It's dependency disguised as devotion. Healthy love doesn't require you to shrink. It doesn't demand that you become less so someone else can feel more. It invites both people to grow side by side, not inside each other's shadows.

Losing yourself in love often starts with good intentions. You want to be easy. You want to be supportive. You want to show that you're all in. But in the process of giving everything, you stop keeping anything for yourself. You make their dreams your mission. You prioritize their comfort over your calling. You start saying "we" when you really mean "I." And even though it feels selfless, it's actually unsustainable. Because the moment that relationship shifts or ends, you're left with an empty space where your identity used to be.

That's why maintaining individuality isn't selfish. It's sacred. It's what allows love to breathe. Two people can't build something lasting if one of them has to disappear for it to work. The healthiest relationships are made up of two whole people who choose each other, not two incomplete people who are trying to become one.

If you've ever looked in the mirror and realized you don't recognize yourself anymore, you know what this feels like. Maybe you've caught yourself agreeing with things you don't believe. Maybe you've let your own dreams sit on the shelf because pursuing them might cause tension. Maybe you've started apologizing for things that aren't even wrong, just to keep harmony. At some point, the peace you thought you were maintaining begins to feel heavy.

Reclaiming yourself after losing your identity in love takes time. It starts with remembering what you liked before you started accommodating. It starts with asking questions like, "What brings me joy that isn't tied to anyone else?" and "What do I need right now that only I can give myself?" It might mean doing things alone again, not to prove independence, but to rebuild self-connection. It might mean setting boundaries that feel uncomfortable because they remind you that you're allowed to take up space.

The most challenging part of this process is realizing that your value never came from how well you loved someone else. It came from the fact that you are already whole, even when you're not attached to anyone. Love is meant to enhance that wholeness, not replace it.

In a healthy relationship, individuality doesn't threaten intimacy. It strengthens it. When both people have room to grow, love expands instead of suffocating. You can show up for your partner without abandoning yourself. You can support their growth without losing sight of your own. You can disagree without disconnecting. That's what mature love looks like.

It's easy to romanticize the idea of being someone's everything, but real love doesn't need you to be everything. It needs you to be real. It needs you to be honest about who you are and what you want. It needs you to bring your full self to the table, not the edited version you think will keep the peace.

If you've spent years defining yourself through someone else, this will feel like starting over. It will feel strange to make decisions without checking how they'll be received. It will feel lonely at times because you've built your identity on connection instead of individuality. But as you begin to find your voice again, you'll notice a different kind of peace. It's quieter, steadier, and not dependent on anyone else's reaction. That's the peace of knowing yourself.

You can love deeply without losing your center. You can give fully without disappearing. The goal is not to stop loving people, but to stop loving them at the expense of yourself. Because the truth is, the more grounded you are in who you are, the more fully you can love. And that's the kind of love that lasts.

Real love doesn't ask you to vanish. It invites you to stand beside someone as your whole self. And when you both do that, the relationship doesn't just survive. It grows stronger, richer, and more honest. It becomes a space where two people can meet in truth rather than merge in fear.

That's the kind of love worth keeping. The kind that lets you be seen without disappearing.

SEVEN

Boundaries Aren't Walls

For most people, the word "boundaries" feels uncomfortable. It sounds harsh, maybe even unkind. We grow up hearing that love means saying yes, being available, and putting others first. Somewhere along the way, we start to believe that drawing lines makes us selfish or cold. So we keep giving, keep stretching, keep absorbing until we reach the point where we have nothing left. Then we call that exhaustion love.

But boundaries are not barriers. They are bridges that make real connection possible. They are the quiet rules that protect your peace so that your love can stay genuine. A boundary doesn't push people away. It shows them where they can safely meet you. Without boundaries, relationships lose clarity. With them, relationships can finally breathe.

When you live without clear boundaries, resentment becomes inevitable. You start to notice yourself feeling drained around certain people but can't quite explain why. You begin to replay conversations in your head, wondering why you said yes again when you knew you wanted to say no. You catch yourself apologizing for needing rest, for wanting space, or for simply being human. That's the price of boundarylessness: you end up managing everyone else's comfort while ignoring your own.

Many of us confuse boundaries with rejection because early in life we were taught that love and compliance go hand in hand. Maybe every time you tried to assert yourself, someone made you feel guilty for it. Maybe you learned that saying no led to tension, so you stopped saying it altogether. Over time, you learned to equate safety with silence. But safety built on silence isn't safety. It's suppression.

A boundary is not a punishment. It's an instruction manual for how to love you well. It says, "Here is where I end and you begin." It tells the truth about what you can give and what you cannot. It allows both people to take responsibility for their own feelings and needs instead of handing that responsibility back and forth like a hot coal.

In my own life, I learned that without boundaries, even good relationships become heavy. I used to think I could manage everyone's moods if I just tried hard enough. I believed I could smooth out tension before it turned into conflict. What I didn't realize was that I was slowly erasing myself in the process. I wasn't protecting love. I was suffocating it.

Once I started setting boundaries, something unexpected happened. The right people respected them. The wrong people resisted them. And that simple truth taught me more about my relationships than any long conversation ever could. People who value control will always push against boundaries because boundaries remove their power. People who value connection will adjust, because they want the relationship to remain healthy.

Setting boundaries will always trigger fear at first. You might worry that you'll lose people. Sometimes you will. But those losses aren't punishment. They're pruning. When a relationship can't survive your honesty, it's not a relationship built on love. It's built on control, and control is the enemy of connection.

Good boundaries don't create distance. They create respect. They allow you to love without resentment. They allow you to rest without guilt. They allow you to give freely because you're no longer giving from depletion. They protect the parts of you that need time to recharge so that when you show up, you show up fully.

Healthy boundaries sound like simple sentences: "I can't talk right now, but I'd love to later." "I want to help, but I don't have the energy tonight." "I care about you, but that conversation isn't healthy for me." They don't require explanation or apology. They are acts of clarity, not conflict.

It's also important to remember that boundaries work both ways. Just as you have the right to set them, others have the right to set theirs. You can't expect someone to respect your limits if you dismiss theirs. Boundaries only create balance when both sides honor them.

If you've lived most of your life without boundaries, this will take practice. You'll have to learn to tolerate guilt without giving in to it. You'll have to remind yourself that discomfort is not danger. You'll have to resist the urge to overexplain or soften your truth. But with each small step, you'll notice a shift. The noise in your relationships quiets. The constant tension fades. You begin to feel more peace, not less.

Boundaries aren't a wall that keeps love out. They are the framework that keeps love safe. They allow you to remain open without being overwhelmed. They teach others how to approach you, not out of fear, but with understanding. And when everyone knows where they stand, connection finally feels stable.

Love without boundaries burns out. Love with boundaries lasts. When you learn to set them, you stop giving from guilt and start giving from grace. You stop proving your worth and start protecting your peace. That's how relationships grow stronger instead of smaller.

Because real love doesn't demand that you have no edges. It asks that you stand firm enough to be trusted.

EIGHT

Relearning How to Receive

For most of my life, I was more comfortable giving than receiving. Compliments, help, support. Anything that required me to stand still and accept made me uneasy. If someone offered to pay for a meal, I'd argue. If someone praised my work, I'd deflect. I thought I was being humble, but the truth is, I just didn't know how to receive.

That realization hit me one night after a long week when a friend showed up at my door with dinner. I hadn't asked for it, but they knew I was worn out. I thanked them, but I felt awkward the entire time we ate. I kept trying to prove I didn't really need it, that I could have handled it myself. When they left, I stood in the doorway and realized something simple but uncomfortable, I had made their gift about me instead of them.

That's what happens when you forget how to receive.

We live in a world that rewards independence. We're told to take pride in being strong, self-sufficient, and capable. Those are good qualities, but somewhere along the way, many of us start believing that needing help makes us weak. We tell ourselves we don't want to burden anyone. We convince ourselves that accepting care is selfish. We hide behind humility when what we really feel is fear.

It's not fear of the gift. It's fear of vulnerability.

To receive is to admit that you have needs. It means opening a door and letting someone step inside. It means surrendering control. For people who have spent their whole lives earning connection through service, that can feel terrifying. You learn to give because giving feels safe. It puts you in control. But receiving requires trust. It asks you to believe that love can come freely, without performance or repayment.

I've seen this pattern in almost everyone who struggles with burnout. They are quick to offer support but slow to accept it. They don't want to inconvenience anyone, but they're already carrying everyone else's weight. They'll drive across town to help a friend move but can't ask for help changing a lightbulb. They think generosity is about constant output, but that's not generosity. That's imbalance.

Healthy relationships are not built on one-way giving. They are built on flow. If you keep pouring without allowing anything to flow back to you, eventually you run dry. Giving and receiving are part of the same current. To block one is to weaken both.

The hardest part of relearning how to receive is letting go of guilt. Somewhere deep down, you may believe you have to earn love, that you must always give first, that accepting kindness without doing something in return is selfish. But love that must be earned isn't love at all. It's transaction. The same way you learned to give freely, you must now learn to receive freely.

Start small. When someone gives you a compliment, don't rush to minimize it. Say thank you. When someone offers to help, let them. When someone reaches out to check on you, don't say "I'm fine" if you're not. Receiving doesn't always mean taking physical help. Sometimes it just means allowing yourself to be seen.

I once worked with a client who said she didn't like asking for help because it made her feel exposed. She said, "If I need something, it means I failed to plan for it." But as we talked, she realized that her need for control came from growing up in a house where asking for help was punished. She learned to survive by being the helper, the reliable one, the person who never needed anything. As an adult, she was still living by that same rule. The moment she started letting people in — even in small ways — she felt like her world expanded. The relationships that had felt shallow suddenly deepened. Her friends said they finally felt closer to her, not because she started doing more, but because she started allowing herself to be human.

That's the irony of learning to receive. The very thing you think will make you a burden often makes people feel more connected to you. Allowing others to give creates intimacy. It gives them the chance to express care in return. It tells them that their presence matters too.

If you've ever been the strong one, the responsible one, the person everyone relies on, this will feel foreign. Your first instinct will be to pull back. You'll want to prove that you can still handle it all. But the truth is, strength without softness becomes isolation. No one can give endlessly without learning to receive.

Receiving isn't passive. It's active trust. It's saying, "I believe you mean this. I trust you enough to accept it." It's allowing love to reach you instead of deflecting it with humor or pride.

If you're not sure where to start, begin with honesty. The next time someone asks if you need anything, resist the reflex to say no. Take a breath. Ask yourself, "What would it feel like to say yes?" Maybe it's not about accepting a big gesture. Maybe it's just about letting someone listen.

Learning to receive doesn't mean you stop giving. It just means you stop controlling how love flows. You stop treating yourself as the only source of care. You start allowing others to play their part in your healing too.

There will be moments when receiving feels uncomfortable. That's normal. It's your nervous system adjusting to a new experience. If you've spent years associating love with effort, resting in it will feel unnatural. But over time, you'll realize that the ability to receive is not a weakness. It's wisdom. It's knowing that you were never meant to carry life alone.

Think about the people you love most. The joy you feel when you help them isn't one-sided. It's mutual. It strengthens the bond. When you refuse to receive, you rob others of that same joy. You deny them the chance to love you in return.

Relearning how to receive is not about asking for more. It's about allowing what's already being offered to reach you. It's about loosening your grip and trusting that love doesn't need to be earned to be real.

And here's the truth that took me far too long to learn — letting someone help you doesn't make you less capable. It makes you more connected.

There's a quiet kind of strength in saying yes. It tells the world, "I don't have to prove my worth by doing everything myself." It tells the people around you, "I trust you enough to let you in."

Giving feels powerful. Receiving feels vulnerable. But love needs both to survive.

So the next time someone offers you kindness, don't argue. Don't explain. Don't try to even the score. Just breathe, look them in the eye, and say, "Thank you."

Because sometimes the most generous thing you can do is simply let yourself be loved.

NINE

Relationship Currency

There was a man I used to work with who had a habit of keeping score. If he bought lunch, he'd mention it every time the check came around. If he did a favor, he made sure everyone knew. On the surface, he looked generous. But over time, I started to see what was really happening. Every act of kindness had a price tag attached.

He didn't give to connect. He gave to collect.

I remember one conversation where he said, "You owe me one," after something small, barely an inconvenience. It stuck with me, because it revealed how many people live like that without realizing it. Relationships, for them, are built on quiet transactions. You do this, so I'll do that. You show up for me, so I'll show up for you. If you don't, we're done.

It sounds cold when you say it out loud, but the truth is that a lot of people approach connection this way. not because they're bad, but because they've learned to see love as a form of currency. They've been taught that value must always be earned and balanced.

When that belief seeps into relationships, it poisons them slowly. Every favor, every call, every gift becomes a mental ledger. You start keeping track of who reached out last, who forgot your birthday, who didn't text back fast enough. You start equating reciprocity with love.

And when people don't return what you gave, it feels like theft.

It's a subtle mindset, but it turns relationships into emotional bookkeeping. Instead of genuine generosity, there's quiet manipulation. Instead of mutual care, there's quiet resentment. You're no longer giving from fullness. You're investing from fear, afraid that if you stop giving, the connection will disappear.

That's not love. That's leverage.

The problem with seeing relationships as transactions is that love doesn't work that way. Real connection can't be balanced like an account. It requires uneven moments. Sometimes you carry more, sometimes they do. Some seasons you're the one pouring, other times you're the one being filled. That flow only works when both people understand that the goal isn't to break even, it's to stay connected.

The deeper truth behind relationship currency is this: when you start keeping score, it's usually because something inside you feels in deficit. You start giving beyond what's healthy to earn validation or security. You offer more than you have, hoping it will guarantee that people won't leave. But the harder you try to earn connection, the less authentic it becomes.

I've done it myself. There was a season where I confused generosity with worth. I thought that if I was always dependable, always available, always helpful, people would love me more. But instead of deepening connection, it quietly drained me. I started to notice that I wasn't giving freely anymore. I was giving out of anxiety. Every favor carried an unspoken hope that it would be noticed, appreciated, and returned.

When it wasn't, I felt used, even though I was the one setting the terms.

That's how the currency trap works. You give to control the outcome, not to connect. You offer love as a transaction instead of a gift. You pretend it's unconditional, but somewhere inside you're waiting for the balance to even out. And when it doesn't, resentment builds.

The worst part is that the people around you can feel it. Even when you never say it out loud, they can sense the expectation behind your kindness. It makes love feel heavy.

If you want to know whether you've fallen into this pattern, pay attention to how you feel after giving. If you feel lighter, it was love. If you feel tense, waiting for something back, it was currency.

That doesn't mean you should keep giving endlessly to people who never reciprocate. Healthy relationships are mutual, not one-sided. But mutuality is not measured by counting favors, it's measured by consistency, trust, and care. The moment you turn love into a contract, it stops being love.

Many people end up here because of past scarcity. Maybe you grew up feeling like affection had to be earned. Maybe someone only showed kindness when you performed well. Maybe you were rewarded for being helpful, or punished for being honest. So as an adult, you try to stay safe by managing emotional exchange. You give to secure. You measure to protect. You withhold to test.

It feels logical, but it's exhausting. Every relationship starts to feel like work.

Breaking that pattern starts with a simple question: *Am I giving to connect, or am I giving to control?*

That question changes everything.

If you're giving to connect, you'll feel peace whether it's returned or not. You're offering something from a place of love, not obligation. But if you're giving to control, you'll feel anxious, tight, or resentful when it isn't noticed. That's the red flag — not that you care too much, but that you're trying to buy what can only be built.

The truth is that love, friendship, and trust all grow through freedom, not transaction. The people who are meant for you don't need to be managed. They'll show up because they want to, not because you bought their loyalty.

When you stop treating connection like currency, you begin to give differently. You stop trying to earn affection. You start to express care because it feels good to give, not because you expect a return. You begin to set boundaries without guilt. You stop chasing validation and start valuing your peace.

You'll still give generously, but now it comes from a full heart instead of an empty one. You'll still help others, but without needing proof that they deserve it. You'll learn to say yes out of joy and no out of honesty.

And you'll start to notice something powerful. The relationships that were built on expectation begin to fade, and the ones built on truth start to deepen. People who were only around for what you provided will quietly drift away. The ones who stay will be the ones who love you for who you are, not what you give.

That shift doesn't just change your relationships, it changes your peace. When you stop keeping score, connection becomes lighter again. You can give without resentment. You can receive without guilt. You can love without fear of losing control.

You'll realize that generosity was never the problem. The problem was the expectation attached to it. Real love doesn't need a receipt. It grows in freedom, not debt.

So give when it's true. Help when it's honest. Be generous when your heart is full. But never spend yourself to buy what's already free.

Because the moment you stop treating love like currency, you remember what it really is — not an exchange to be managed, but an overflow to be shared.

TEN

The Language of Listening

Most people think they are good listeners. They nod at the right times, give advice when asked, and try to show that they care. But listening is not the same as waiting for your turn to speak. It's not about fixing or responding. It's about understanding. It's about hearing what someone means, not just what they say.

Good listening requires more than open ears. It requires an open heart. It asks you to set aside your need to be right or to be helpful long enough to truly absorb what the other person is trying to share. That sounds simple, but it isn't. Because real listening means you have to be fully present. You can't do that while planning your rebuttal or thinking about what to say next. You can't do that while trying to solve the problem before you've heard the whole story.

In most relationships, poor listening is one of the first things to break down. People start talking past each other instead of to each other. One person speaks from pain, the other hears it as criticism. One person asks for comfort, the other offers solutions. Both walk away feeling unseen, even though words were exchanged. It's not that either person is bad at communicating. It's that both are listening through filters instead of curiosity.

Those filters come from experience. If you grew up feeling unheard, you'll listen defensively, waiting for the moment you're misunderstood. If you were taught that being right is safer than being vulnerable, you'll listen for errors, not emotions. If you associate disagreement with danger, you'll listen for warning signs instead of meaning. The result is predictable. Conversations turn into competitions. Instead of listening to connect, you listen to protect.

The language of listening begins when you stop assuming you already know what someone means. It's the difference between reacting and receiving. When someone shares something with you, especially something difficult, the most powerful response is not advice. It's attention. It's giving them the gift of feeling understood.

You can hear someone say, "I'm fine," and know they're not, but you can only know that if you're actually paying attention. You can notice the shift in their tone, the hesitation in their voice, the way their eyes move away at the hardest part of the story. True listening happens not just with your ears but with your awareness. It requires patience, empathy, and the humility to realize that understanding someone doesn't mean agreeing with them.

The hardest part of listening well is learning to stay quiet. Most people fill silence because they mistake it for discomfort. But silence is often where truth settles. When you resist the urge to interrupt, people begin to trust you with their deeper thoughts. They start saying what they actually mean instead of what they think you can handle. Silence tells them that you have space for their truth.

Listening also means releasing the need to fix. Sometimes, the person speaking doesn't want a solution. They want a witness. They want to know they're not crazy for feeling what they feel. They want to know someone else can sit with their pain without turning away. That kind of listening is powerful because it offers presence instead of pressure.

In your own life, notice how often you listen to respond. It happens everywhere. In friendships, marriages, workplaces, even parenting. We jump to defend, explain, or justify because it feels safer than staying still. But what if the goal wasn't to win the conversation? What if the goal was simply to understand?

Learning the language of listening also means recognizing how you want to be heard. When you speak, what do you wish others would do? Most people want patience, attention, and empathy. If that's what you crave, start giving it. When you model what good listening looks like, others begin to mirror it back. Relationships slowly shift.

When listening becomes the priority, everything changes. Conflicts that used to explode begin to soften. People who were guarded start to open up. You stop needing to convince anyone, because they finally feel seen. You start to realize that being understood is far more healing than being agreed with.

Listening is love in its quietest form. It says, "You matter enough for me to slow down and be here." It asks for nothing in return. It doesn't measure, calculate, or compare. It simply allows space for another person to be human.

You don't have to be perfect at it. You just have to care enough to try. Because when you learn the language of listening, you stop hearing words and start hearing hearts. And that is where real connection begins.

ELEVEN

Conflict Without Collapse

Conflict is a part of every relationship. You can avoid it, postpone it, or pretend it doesn't exist, but sooner or later it finds you. And when it does, it exposes the truth about how strong your connection really is. Healthy relationships don't avoid conflict. They learn how to walk through it without falling apart.

Most of us were never taught how to do that. We were taught to win arguments, not to understand people. We were taught that being right keeps us safe, that apologizing means losing, and that silence keeps the peace. Those lessons might have helped us survive in certain environments, but they make intimacy almost impossible. Because closeness requires honesty, and honesty always creates friction.

The goal in conflict is not to eliminate tension. It's to learn how to stay present within it. The moment a disagreement becomes a threat, most people go into one of two modes: they fight harder or they shut down. Both reactions are forms of self-protection. One attacks to regain control. The other retreats to avoid pain. Neither creates resolution.

When you can stay grounded in conflict, everything changes. You stop seeing the other person as an enemy and start seeing them as someone who is hurting or trying to be heard. You begin to understand that anger is often just fear in disguise. Disappointment is usually grief. Defensiveness is protection. Once you recognize that, the conversation shifts from accusation to understanding.

Learning how to do this starts with slowing down. When emotions rise, your body reacts before your brain does. Your heart races, your chest tightens, your thoughts scramble. It feels like you need to fix it immediately, but that urgency usually makes things worse. Instead of responding, take a breath. Remind yourself that conflict is not a crisis. It's information. It's a signal that something in the relationship needs attention.

Most of the time, the surface issue isn't the real issue. The fight about being late is rarely about time. It's about feeling disrespected. The argument about chores isn't about the dishes. It's about feeling unseen. When you focus on being right, you miss the deeper message. But when you focus on understanding, you can finally get to the heart of what's wrong.

In conflict, listening matters more than logic. You can prove your point and still lose the relationship. You can win the argument and still feel lonely. Resolution isn't about convincing someone you're right. It's about restoring connection. The question to ask isn't "Who's to blame?" but "What are we both trying to protect?"

There will be moments when staying calm feels impossible. You'll feel the urge to defend yourself or to withdraw completely. That's normal. The key is to notice it without judgment. Step back mentally before you react verbally. You can always return to the conversation later. Sometimes the healthiest thing you can say is, "I need a moment to gather my thoughts before I respond." That pause is not avoidance. It's maturity.

Another truth about conflict is that resolution doesn't always mean agreement. Two people can understand each other deeply and still see things differently. The goal isn't perfect alignment. It's mutual respect. When both people feel heard, the argument loses its power. What remains is understanding, and understanding is what builds trust.

You can tell a lot about a relationship by how it handles conflict. When people care about each other, they don't aim to destroy. They aim to repair. They ask questions instead of making accusations. They use "I feel" instead of "You always." They stay in the conversation, not to win, but to connect.

Sometimes, despite your best effort, conflict will still end badly. Words will be said that can't be taken back. Distance will happen. That doesn't mean the relationship is ruined. It means both people have work to do. Healing often happens in the space after the argument, when both sides have time to reflect. What matters most is what you do with that reflection. Do you come back defensive, or do you come back humble? Do you focus on proving, or do you focus on peace?

When you start viewing conflict as a tool instead of a threat, relationships become stronger. Disagreements no longer scare you. You begin to see them as checkpoints that test whether your connection can handle truth. You realize that every argument is an opportunity to practice honesty, empathy, and restraint.

Healthy conflict doesn't destroy love. It reveals it. It shows whether both people can handle truth without withdrawing it. It asks whether the bond is strong enough to hold two perspectives at once. And when it is, the relationship grows deeper, steadier, and more real.

Conflict without collapse doesn't mean perfection. It means the courage to stay, listen, and repair, even when it's uncomfortable. It means valuing connection more than control. Because at the end of the day, love is not proven by how often you agree. It's proven by how well you reconcile when you don't.

TWELVE

Expectations and Invisible Contracts

Every relationship runs on expectations. Some are spoken, some are not. The spoken ones are simple. You expect honesty, respect, consistency. The unspoken ones are trickier. You expect them to know what you need without being told. You expect them to respond how you would respond. You expect them to notice what you notice, care how you care, and love the way you love. Those expectations are rarely intentional, but they create invisible contracts that shape how we interact.

Invisible contracts are the promises we think someone has made, even though they never actually did. They sound like, "If I'm always there for you, you'll be there for me." Or "If I love you enough, you'll change." Or "If I stay calm, you'll stay kind." None of those agreements are real, but we build our emotional security on them as if they are. When those expectations go unmet, we feel betrayed. We tell ourselves they broke the contract, when the truth is, they never signed it in the first place.

This dynamic is one of the most common sources of frustration in relationships. It's the gap between what you believe should happen and what actually does. That gap breeds disappointment, resentment, and confusion. We start thinking the other person is selfish or careless when, in reality, they're just unaware. You can't hold someone accountable for a rule they didn't know existed.

The only way to close that gap is through communication. But communication takes courage. It means admitting that your needs are not being met and that you want something to change. For many people, that honesty feels risky. We fear that if we ask for too much, we'll seem needy. So instead of speaking up, we stay quiet and hope the other person will eventually figure it out. They don't. And every time they miss the mark, our resentment grows.

I used to think that if someone really loved me, they would just know what I needed. I thought love meant mind reading. But love is not telepathy. It's transparency. When you clearly express your expectations, you give people the opportunity to meet them. When you hide those expectations, you set them up to fail.

It helps to remember that everyone has a different idea of what "normal" looks like. What feels obvious to you might never occur to someone else. You might think "checking in every day" is a basic sign of care, while someone else sees it as unnecessary pressure. You might believe that "quality time" means long conversations, while the other person believes it means shared silence. Neither is wrong. But unless you talk about it, both will feel misunderstood.

One of the most common invisible contracts shows up in giving. You give your time, your attention, your energy, and deep down, you expect equal effort in return. When it doesn't come, you start keeping score. That's not generosity anymore. That's quiet accounting. If you give something only because you hope to get something back, it stops being a gift. True giving releases the outcome. Anything else becomes a trade.

To break free from invisible contracts, you have to start naming what you need. That sounds simple, but it takes practice. It means saying things like, "When you cancel plans last minute, I feel unimportant." Or "When you go silent during arguments, I feel abandoned." It's not about blame. It's about clarity. Clarity creates safety because everyone knows what's real instead of guessing what's wrong.

Sometimes, when you start speaking honestly, people will surprise you. They'll rise to the occasion because they genuinely want to love you better. Other times, they'll show you they can't or won't. Both outcomes are valuable. They tell you what kind of relationship you actually have, not the one you were pretending existed.

Setting expectations also requires looking inward. You need to ask yourself whether what you expect is fair or rooted in fantasy. Are you asking someone to meet a need that really belongs to you? Are you expecting them to fill a void that communication or self-awareness could solve? Healthy expectations are specific, mutual, and realistic. Unhealthy ones are vague, one-sided, and built on hope instead of truth.

If you want to know whether you're holding invisible contracts, look for your resentment. Resentment is often the evidence of an unspoken expectation. It's the emotional receipt for an agreement the other person never signed. Instead of collecting more of those receipts, pause and ask yourself, "Have I actually told them what I need?" If the answer is no, that's your next step.

The healthiest relationships are the ones where nothing important stays unspoken. Where people feel safe enough to tell the truth before it turns into tension. Where expectations aren't weapons used to test loyalty, but shared understandings that make love easier.

When you bring invisible contracts into the light, they lose their power. What used to feel confusing becomes clear. What used to feel personal becomes practical. And slowly, the pressure that once strained the relationship begins to fade.

The truth is, no one can meet your expectations perfectly. But with honesty, patience, and compassion, you can build relationships where both people are free to try without fear of failing. That's how trust grows. That's how resentment dies. That's how love becomes real again.

THIRTEEN

The Fear of Depth

Everyone wants connection, but not everyone is ready for what it requires. True closeness asks for depth, and depth asks for vulnerability. That's where many people quietly pull back. They want to be known, but not fully. They want honesty, but only the kind that doesn't expose too much. They want love, but only if it doesn't demand change. It's not that they don't care. It's that somewhere along the line, they learned that being open is dangerous.

The fear of depth is one of the most common barriers to real connection. It doesn't always show up as fear. Sometimes it looks like independence. Sometimes it looks like humor or distraction. Sometimes it looks like control. The pattern is simple. When things start to feel emotionally real, you find a way to retreat. You change the subject. You minimize your feelings. You distract with logic. Anything to avoid the risk of being seen.

This fear almost always comes from experience. Maybe you opened up once and it was used against you. Maybe you were made to feel weak for having needs. Maybe you learned early that showing emotion led to rejection or shame. Over time, you stopped reaching for depth because shallow felt safer. You convinced yourself that distance was strength.

The problem is, you can't have intimacy without exposure. You can't be fully loved without being fully known. You can't feel genuine connection while hiding behind your armor. You might stay protected, but you'll stay lonely too. Surface-level relationships can keep you entertained, but they will never make you feel seen.

Depth is risky because it removes your control. Once you reveal your fears, your insecurities, or your truth, you no longer get to manage how others perceive you. You can only hope they handle it with care. That lack of control terrifies people who have been hurt before. But what if the point isn't to guarantee safety? What if the point is to practice courage?

Courage in relationships doesn't mean oversharing or spilling everything all at once. It means allowing yourself to be authentic, even when it's uncomfortable. It means saying, "I'm not okay," instead of pretending you are. It means admitting when you're scared, when you need help, when you've been hurt. Vulnerability is not weakness. It's evidence that you are alive and willing to engage with life honestly.

One of the easiest ways to see the fear of depth is in how people handle silence. Shallow connections rush to fill every quiet space. Deep ones can sit in it. They can let the stillness speak. They can let the truth breathe. Silence is uncomfortable only when you're trying to hide. When you're comfortable with yourself, silence feels sacred.

Relationships built on depth require patience. You can't force someone to meet you there if they're not ready. You also can't keep lowering yourself to meet them at the surface. Depth grows when both people create space for honesty and safety at the same time. It happens when you listen without judgment and speak without performance. It happens when you allow conversations to go beyond logistics and opinions and enter into feelings, fears, and dreams.

There is always a moment in every relationship when you hit a choice point. You can stay safe or you can go deep. Going deep means you risk rejection. Staying safe means you guarantee distance. Most people choose safety, but safety without connection eventually becomes isolation. You might avoid heartbreak, but you also avoid belonging.

If you have lived guarded for a long time, the first steps toward depth will feel foreign. You'll question your timing. You'll wonder if it's worth it. You'll feel exposed. But with time, you start to realize that depth doesn't destroy relationships. It defines them. The people who are meant to stay will meet you there. The ones who are not will drift away. Either outcome gives you truth.

Depth isn't about intensity. It's about honesty. It's not measured by how dramatic or emotional you can be. It's measured by how real you are willing to become. Can you be yourself without editing? Can you sit with someone else's truth without trying to fix it? Can you stay when things get uncomfortable instead of running to what feels easy? Those are the moments that separate connection from contact.

The fear of depth fades only when you stop trying to avoid pain and start learning from it. When you realize that being hurt is survivable but living numb is not. When you see that discomfort isn't danger but a sign that you are stepping into truth. Depth isn't about never being afraid. It's about choosing to show up anyway.

The more you practice it, the more natural it becomes. You'll notice that your conversations start to change. They become slower, more meaningful, less performative. You'll stop needing every interaction to feel perfect and start valuing the ones that feel honest. You'll stop chasing connection and start creating it.

Because depth is not something you find. It's something you allow. It's what happens when you stop protecting yourself from being seen and start letting yourself be known. And when you do, the relationships in your life begin to reflect that same openness back to you.

That's when you realize that depth was never the threat. Avoidance was.

FOURTEEN

The Maintenance Gap

Relationships rarely end because of one big event. Most of the time, they erode slowly. Not from betrayal, not from anger, but from neglect. It happens quietly, almost invisibly. One person stops checking in. The other stops reaching out. Small misunderstandings go unspoken. Little disappointments stack up. Days turn into weeks, and eventually the connection that once felt alive becomes something that only exists in memory.

This slow decay is what I call the maintenance gap. It's the space between the effort a relationship needs and the effort it actually receives. Every relationship requires upkeep. Just like anything else you care about, it needs attention, intention, and time. Yet many people treat relationships like self-sustaining systems. They assume love, friendship, or trust will continue running on their own, even without regular investment. They won't.

At the beginning of any connection, maintenance feels effortless. You want to check in. You want to listen. You want to spend time together. But as familiarity grows, effort fades. The urgency to connect gets replaced by routine. The attention you once gave naturally now requires thought. It's not that you stop caring. It's that you stop noticing.

This is one of the most common reasons relationships drift. People confuse comfort with stability. They believe that because things are calm, they must also be healthy. But calm can sometimes mean distance. Silence can sometimes mean disconnection. Familiarity can make you lazy. When something feels secure, you stop feeding it, forgetting that even secure things die when neglected.

The maintenance gap widens gradually. It starts with small dismissals. You skim through a conversation instead of really listening. You assume the other person knows you care, so you stop saying it out loud. You tell yourself you'll spend more time together "when things slow down," but they never do. Over time, what used to be connection turns into coexistence.

This doesn't just happen in romantic relationships. It happens in friendships, families, and even work partnerships. The best relationships are not the ones that never experience distance. They are the ones where both people notice the distance and choose to close it. That choice is what keeps love alive.

The maintenance gap also reveals the difference between intention and attention. Most people have good intentions. They mean to call. They mean to listen. They mean to be more present. But relationships don't grow from intentions. They grow from attention. Love lives in the small, consistent moments. The text that says, "I'm thinking of you." The question that goes deeper than "How are you?" The decision to put your phone down when someone is speaking.

It's easy to underestimate the power of these small acts, but they are what hold relationships together. Grand gestures might create excitement, but consistency builds trust. When people feel consistently seen, they relax. When they relax, they open. And when they open, the connection deepens.

If you've noticed a maintenance gap in one of your relationships, it's not too late to repair it. Start by acknowledging it. Say, "I miss how we used to connect." Don't make it a blame conversation. Make it a bridge conversation. Then take one small action to close the gap. Schedule a walk. Make time for an uninterrupted conversation. Write a message that doesn't need a reply. Every effort counts.

The truth is, relationships don't fall apart because people stop loving each other. They fall apart because people stop tending to the love. They assume that once something feels strong, it will stay that way. But strength without maintenance eventually weakens. Even the healthiest connections need care.

It's important to remember that maintenance doesn't mean perfection. You don't have to constantly talk or always agree. You just have to stay aware. When something feels off, address it. When someone feels distant, reach out. When the energy feels uneven, rebalance it. Maintenance is about presence, not performance.

The maintenance gap is a quiet thief. It takes what is beautiful and turns it into background noise. The good news is that awareness is enough to stop it. Relationships can be revived. Trust can be rebuilt. Closeness can return. It starts with one person deciding to pay attention again.

Love is a living thing. If you stop feeding it, it fades. But the moment you start nurturing it again, it remembers how to grow. Every check-in, every apology, every small act of care adds up. Over time, those little things rebuild what neglect tried to erase.

Closing the maintenance gap doesn't require grand effort. It requires simple, steady commitment. It means refusing to take connection for granted. It means remembering that love isn't a one-time promise. It's a daily practice.

The relationships that last are not the ones without problems. They are the ones that keep being maintained.

FIFTEEN

Seasons and Cycles

Every relationship has a life cycle. Some enter your story to teach you a lesson. Some arrive to walk with you for a while. Some stay for the long haul. The problem is that most people expect every connection to last forever, and when it doesn't, they see it as failure. But not every relationship is meant to be permanent. Some are meant to be purposeful.

The idea that people come into your life for a reason, a season, or a lifetime is simple, but it holds deep truth. Each connection plays a part in shaping who you become. When you learn to recognize which kind of relationship you're in, you stop holding on out of habit and start appreciating people for the role they were meant to play.

Reason relationships are the ones that arrive at exactly the right time. They bring a lesson, a challenge, or a change you didn't even know you needed. Sometimes they awaken something in you. Sometimes they break something open that had to be healed. They are often intense and short-lived. They might not last, but their impact does. These relationships teach you something essential about yourself, even if the lesson is hard. They remind you that growth rarely feels gentle.

Season relationships last longer. They are built around shared time, shared purpose, or shared circumstance. You might meet a friend who helps you navigate a specific phase of your life. You might have a mentor who guides you through a chapter of growth. You might have a partner who fits the person you were at a certain time but not the person you are becoming. These relationships matter deeply, but they are not meant to last forever. Their value is found in the season they serve.

Lifetime relationships are rare. They evolve with you. They weather change, distance, and difficulty. They require effort, honesty, and forgiveness. Lifetime connections aren't perfect, but they are enduring. They don't hold you back from growth; they grow with you. When you find one, it becomes less about maintaining perfection and more about maintaining presence.

The challenge is that most people don't know how to let go when a reason or season comes to an end. We cling to the idea of what was because it feels safer than facing what is. We confuse comfort with connection. We tell ourselves that history is the same as harmony. But holding on to something that has already served its purpose doesn't preserve it. It slowly erodes it.

Learning to release with grace is one of the hardest parts of showing up relationally. It requires gratitude instead of resentment. It requires acceptance instead of resistance. It means saying, "I'm thankful for what this was, and I no longer need it to be something it's not." That kind of release isn't rejection. It's recognition. It honors what was real without forcing it to stay beyond its time.

I have learned that not every ending is a loss. Sometimes, endings are evidence of growth. When you outgrow a connection, it doesn't mean you've failed. It means you've evolved. And sometimes the most loving thing you can do for both people is to let go. You don't have to shut the door with anger. You can close it quietly, with respect and peace.

There will always be people who struggle to understand this. They'll think that love must always mean longevity. But love doesn't always mean staying. Sometimes love means releasing someone to follow their path while you continue on yours. It means trusting that what was shared was enough. It means believing that endings can be sacred too.

The seasons and cycles of relationships mirror the rhythm of life itself. Spring brings new beginnings. Summer brings joy and growth. Autumn brings reflection and change. Winter brings rest and closure. You cannot hold on to summer forever, no matter how much you love the warmth. Each season has its beauty, and each one prepares you for the next.

When you understand that relationships work the same way, you stop trying to make everything permanent. You stop forcing what has already faded. You learn to meet people where they are instead of where you wish they would stay. You learn to appreciate presence while it lasts, instead of fearing its end.

Every person who enters your life leaves something behind. Some leave lessons. Some leave laughter. Some leave love. None of it is wasted. When you look back, you'll see that each relationship added something essential to your story. Even the painful ones served a purpose. They taught you how to stand, how to heal, how to see yourself more clearly.

The beauty of relationships is not in their length but in their authenticity. A short, honest connection can change you more than a long, superficial one. A friendship that ends well can still be a success. A relationship that no longer fits can still be cherished.

Learning to honor the reason, the season, and the lifetime frees you from bitterness. It helps you hold gratitude instead of guilt. It helps you love people as they are instead of trying to make them stay how they were. And it allows you to trust that what's meant for you will last, not because you forced it, but because it's built to.

Every ending is also an invitation. It asks you to look around and notice who is walking with you now, who you might have overlooked, who might be entering your life for their own reason or season. When you learn to see relationships this way, you stop fearing change and start trusting the rhythm of connection.

Because love, in all its forms, was never meant to be controlled. It was meant to be experienced, appreciated, and, when the time comes, released with grace.

SIXTEEN

Knowing When to Let Go

Letting go is one of the hardest parts of any relationship. It goes against our nature to release what once felt safe. We hold on because we remember the good moments, the laughter, the feeling of belonging. We replay old memories and convince ourselves that if we just try harder, things will go back to how they used to be. But sometimes, the truth is not that something went wrong. It's that something ran its course.

Knowing when to let go is not about giving up easily. It's about recognizing when holding on is doing more harm than good. It's about being honest with yourself when the relationship you're fighting to save no longer exists in the form you remember. You can't heal what refuses to grow, and you can't grow if you refuse to accept what is.

The signs that it's time to let go rarely arrive all at once. They come as quiet discomforts. Conversations start to feel forced. You begin editing yourself to avoid conflict. You walk away from interactions feeling smaller instead of seen. The warmth that once drew you together is replaced by tension, or worse, indifference. It doesn't mean either person is bad. It just means the connection has stopped aligning with who you're becoming.

The hardest part about letting go is the guilt. We tell ourselves that good people don't walk away. We confuse loyalty with self-abandonment. We believe that leaving means failure. But staying in something that no longer nurtures you isn't loyalty. It's fear. It's the belief that suffering is somehow more noble than peace.

Every relationship will have hard seasons, but not every hard season means the relationship should end. The difference lies in effort. If both people are still showing up, still trying to communicate, still willing to grow, there is always hope. But if only one person is fighting to keep it alive, the relationship has already shifted into imbalance. One person can't carry what was meant for two.

Letting go doesn't always mean cutting someone out completely. Sometimes it means releasing the expectation of what they were supposed to be. It means accepting that the version of them you loved may no longer exist, and that the healthiest way forward is to meet them where they are now, not where they were then. It means creating space for the relationship to evolve, even if that evolution looks like distance.

The process of letting go begins with honesty. You have to tell the truth about what's actually happening, not what you wish was happening. You have to stop explaining away the patterns that keep repeating. You have to look at the relationship as it is, not as it used to be. That honesty will hurt at first, but it's also what makes healing possible.

Once you acknowledge the truth, grief follows. Grieving someone who is still alive is one of the strangest kinds of pain. You mourn the connection, the familiarity, and the version of yourself that existed within it. It's okay to miss it. It's okay to cry over what's ending even if you know it's right. Letting go with love means allowing yourself to feel the loss fully, without bitterness.

Eventually, you start to feel something new in that space. Relief. You realize that peace was waiting on the other side of your resistance. You notice that your body feels lighter. You start sleeping better. You start hearing your own thoughts again. That's what happens when you stop clinging to something that was draining you. The energy you used to spend holding it together becomes available for growth, creativity, and joy.

Letting go also doesn't erase the good that came from the relationship. You can honor what it gave you. You can carry the lessons without carrying the weight. You can love someone deeply and still accept that you can't continue in the same way. Love doesn't always mean staying. Sometimes it means releasing.

If you find yourself in the middle of a relationship that feels uncertain, ask yourself a few honest questions. Do I feel more myself or less when I'm with this person? Do I leave our interactions feeling seen or diminished? Are we both growing, or am I the only one trying? Am I staying out of love or out of fear? The answers won't always be simple, but they will be clear if you're willing to listen.

There is grace in walking away well. You don't need to destroy what was good just because it's ending. You don't need to justify your decision with anger. You can leave quietly, with gratitude for the time shared. You can wish someone well without wishing them back. That kind of ending takes maturity. It also brings peace.

Letting go is an act of faith. It's trusting that what's ahead can be just as meaningful as what's behind. It's believing that endings are not failures, but transitions. When you release something with love instead of resentment, you make room for something new to grow in its place.

You are not betraying anyone by choosing peace. You are honoring the truth. And when you honor the truth, you give both yourself and the other person the freedom to become who you were always meant to be.

So when it's time to let go, do it gently. Do it honestly. Do it without bitterness. Thank the relationship for what it gave you, bless it for what it taught you, and step forward knowing that endings, too, are sacred.

SEVENTEEN

Healing From Relational Wounds

Every person carries scars from relationships. Some are visible. Others live quietly beneath the surface, shaping how we love, trust, and show up. These wounds can come from anywhere. A parent who never listened. A friend who disappeared when you needed them most. A partner who betrayed your trust. The details change, but the effect is the same. Something in you learns to be careful.

Relational wounds don't heal just because time passes. They heal when we learn to face them. The challenge is that most people try to move on too quickly. They bury the pain under distraction or convince themselves that it doesn't matter anymore. But pain that isn't processed doesn't disappear. It hides, waiting for the next relationship to trigger it again.

That is why similar patterns keep showing up. The wound is calling for attention.

Healing starts with honesty. You have to be willing to admit that something hurt you, even if you think you should be over it by now. Minimizing your pain doesn't make you strong. It keeps you stuck. Acknowledging what happened doesn't mean blaming others forever. It means allowing yourself to feel the truth of what you experienced. Only then can you begin to release it.

The next step is understanding the impact. Every wound leaves behind a belief. You might start believing that people can't be trusted, or that you have to perform to be loved, or that closeness always leads to disappointment. These beliefs feel like protection, but they become prisons. They limit what you allow yourself to receive. They keep love at a distance because they make you believe you're safer alone.

To heal, you have to challenge those beliefs. You have to ask, "Is this still true, or is this just familiar?" Often, it's the familiarity that feels safe, not the truth. You might feel drawn to relationships that recreate your old pain because they match the emotional pattern you know best. It's not that you want to suffer. It's that your nervous system confuses predictability with peace. Healing requires breaking that pattern, even when it feels uncomfortable.

Forgiveness is also part of healing, but it's often misunderstood. Forgiveness doesn't mean pretending it didn't happen or excusing someone's behavior. It means releasing the power that pain has over you. It means deciding that the story doesn't get to define you anymore. Forgiveness is not about the other person. It's about freeing yourself. You can forgive someone and still never speak to them again. You can let go without reopening a door.

Another piece of healing is learning to rebuild trust. This takes time, and it starts with yourself. Trust yourself to see red flags sooner. Trust yourself to speak up when something feels wrong. Trust yourself to walk away when a pattern returns. When you start honoring your own signals, you stop depending on others to protect you from pain. You become your own safe place.

Rebuilding trust with others comes slowly. It doesn't happen through grand gestures or perfect apologies. It happens through small, consistent actions. It happens when someone listens instead of defending. When they show up when it's inconvenient. When they admit mistakes instead of hiding them. You'll know it's safe again not when the fear disappears, but when the effort outweighs the fear.

Healing from relational wounds also means allowing yourself to receive love again. After being hurt, it's tempting to stay guarded. You tell yourself that you're protecting your heart, but what you're really doing is keeping it closed. Protection can become isolation if you never open the gate. Learning to receive again is an act of courage. It means risking disappointment for the possibility of connection. It means believing that not everyone will repeat the same story.

Some days, healing will feel like progress. Other days, it will feel like you've gone backward. That's normal. Healing is rarely linear. What matters is that you keep showing up for yourself through it. Be patient with your own process. Grief takes time. So does trust. So does learning how to love again after pain.

You will know you are healing when your memories no longer hurt the same way. When you can think about what happened without feeling like you're back in it. When you can see the lesson without reliving the wound. You will start to notice that you no longer feel the need to rehearse the story for validation. You've made peace with it. You've learned what it came to teach.

And then one day, without realizing it, you'll meet someone who treats you differently. They'll listen instead of dismiss. They'll stay when things get uncomfortable. They'll make you feel calm instead of anxious. When that happens, part of you will want to run, because peace feels foreign. Stay. Let yourself experience what safety feels like. That's when you'll know the wound has become wisdom.

Healing from relational wounds doesn't erase your past. It transforms it. It turns pain into perspective. It turns fear into discernment. It teaches you how to love again with open eyes and a steady heart. You begin to trust not because everyone is safe, but because you know you are strong enough to handle what comes.

Pain changes you. Healing refines you. Both shape who you become. But the real freedom comes when you can look back and thank the wound for what it taught you, not because you

needed the hurt, but because you needed the growth that
came from it.

That is what healing really is. It's not the absence of scars. It's
the presence of peace.

EIGHTEEN

Showing Up for Friends

Friendship is one of the most underrated forms of love. It rarely gets the attention that romance or family does, yet it often shapes us just as deeply. A good friend can change the way you see yourself. A bad one can leave scars that take years to understand. Friendship holds a mirror to who we are when no one is watching. It asks whether we can give and receive without expectation. It asks whether we can be loyal without losing ourselves.

Most people say they value friendship, but few know how to nurture it well. The truth is that friendships require the same care, honesty, and boundaries as any other relationship. They don't survive on history alone. They need maintenance. They need effort. They need presence. Without those things, even the strongest connection can quietly fade.

Showing up for friends starts with consistency. You don't have to be available every day, but you do have to be dependable. Friendship isn't about constant communication. It's about trust. It's knowing that when life gets hard, you have people who will show up, and that you'll do the same. It's not the number of texts or calls that keep a friendship alive. It's the sense that someone genuinely cares.

A healthy friendship is built on balance. Both people give. Both receive. Both feel safe to speak honestly without fear of judgment. When one person is always the listener and the other is always the one in crisis, imbalance grows. Eventually, the friendship begins to feel like work instead of connection. The best friendships are not about fixing each other. They are about holding space for each other.

To show up for a friend, you don't always need the right words. You just need to be present. Sometimes that means sitting in silence. Sometimes it means showing up at their door with food. Sometimes it means sending a simple message that says, "I'm thinking of you." People rarely remember perfect advice, but they never forget how you made them feel.

Friendship also asks for honesty. Real friends tell each other the truth, even when it's uncomfortable. They don't enable harmful patterns out of fear of losing the relationship. They don't gossip behind each other's backs. They don't pretend everything is fine when it's not. They care enough to speak with compassion and enough humility to listen in return.

Boundaries are just as important in friendships as in romance. You can love someone deeply and still say no. You can support them without fixing their problems. You can give them space when they need it and ask for space when you do. A boundary in friendship protects both people from burnout and resentment. It allows care to remain genuine instead of obligatory.

Another part of showing up is learning to celebrate. Too often, friendships are strong during hard times but fragile during good ones. It's easy to show compassion when someone is hurting. It's harder to stay supportive when they're succeeding. A true friend doesn't compete. They cheer. They are not threatened by your growth. They are inspired by it.

Friendship also evolves over time. Some friends will walk with you for years. Others will only stay for a chapter. You don't need to label every change as loss. People grow in different directions, and that's okay. The mark of a mature friendship is the ability to let it shift without bitterness. You can hold gratitude for what was even as you make space for what's next.

Of course, not all friendships are easy. Some will disappoint you. Some will fade no matter how much effort you give. When that happens, don't let it harden you. Every connection, even the painful ones, teaches you something about loyalty, forgiveness, or discernment. Let it make you wiser, not colder.

If you've been hurt by friends before, it can feel risky to open up again. You might keep people at a distance out of fear that they'll leave or betray you. But real friendship requires vulnerability. It asks you to believe that there are still good people who will meet your effort with their own. When you find those people, hold them close.

To show up for friends is to live with intention. It's remembering birthdays and milestones. It's checking in even when there's no crisis. It's telling someone you're proud of them. It's forgiving mistakes without keeping score. It's saying, "I'm here," and meaning it.

You don't need a large circle to feel supported. You just need a few people who see you clearly and love you anyway. Friendship isn't about how many people you know. It's about how deeply you know them.

So keep showing up. Keep reaching out. Keep tending to the friendships that feel mutual, kind, and real. Because at the end of the day, success, healing, and even love mean very little without someone to share them with.

The older you get, the more you realize that true friendship is not built on convenience. It's built on commitment. It's built on being there when it counts. It's built on the simple, sacred truth that no one should have to walk through life alone.

NINETEEN

Family, History, and the Weight of Expectation

Family is often where we learn our first lessons about love, belonging, and identity. It is also where we learn some of our most complicated habits. Family shapes how we communicate, how we handle conflict, and how we define success. It can be a source of comfort or pain, stability or tension. For most people, it's a mix of all those things at once.

No relationship carries more invisible pressure than the ones we have with family. We want their approval. We want their respect. We want them to see us for who we've become instead of who we used to be. Yet, for many, family is also where they feel the least understood. Old roles and expectations can follow you long after you've outgrown them. You might be an adult now, but around your family, you still feel like the child trying to prove something.

These old roles can be hard to break. Maybe you were always the responsible one, the peacekeeper, or the problem solver. Maybe you were the one who stayed quiet so others could stay comfortable. Or maybe you were the rebel, the one everyone blamed for disrupting the calm. Whatever your role was, it can still shape how you show up today. You might find yourself reacting out of habit instead of intention. You might find yourself seeking validation from people who may never give it.

The truth is that growing up means learning to redefine family in a way that protects your peace. You can love your family deeply and still decide to relate to them differently. You can honor where you came from without repeating the patterns that hurt you. You can set boundaries without disrespect. That balance takes maturity. It means letting go of the fantasy that your family will suddenly become who you wish they were and instead learning how to engage with who they actually are.

One of the hardest lessons in family relationships is realizing that love does not always equal understanding. Someone can love you and still not get you. They might not understand your choices, your boundaries, or your healing. They might even take your growth personally. When that happens, you have to decide which matters more: being understood or being at peace. Sometimes, you cannot have both.

Family expectations run deep. They can influence your career, your beliefs, and even how you think about success. You might feel pressure to live a certain way to make your parents proud. You might feel guilty for wanting something different from what everyone else wanted. But living under the weight of family expectations eventually suffocates your individuality. You were not created to be a reflection of anyone else's unfinished dreams. You were created to live your own.

Breaking those expectations doesn't mean you stop loving your family. It means you start loving yourself enough to live honestly. It might look like pursuing a path they don't understand. It might mean limiting time with relatives who drain you instead of support you. It might mean saying no to obligations that feel more like performances than connection. These choices don't make you ungrateful. They make you healthy.

Sometimes, healing within family means accepting that reconciliation might not look like closeness. For some people, peace comes through distance. For others, it comes through boundaries that create room for mutual respect. Not every relationship can return to what it was, and that's okay. You can still wish someone well from afar. You can still love them without letting them have access to the parts of you that they keep wounding.

It's also true that family can surprise you. The same people who once didn't understand might grow. They might soften over time. They might start to see you differently when you stop trying to prove yourself and simply live your truth.

Change doesn't always happen quickly, but sometimes your consistency inspires it. When you stop arguing and start modeling peace, others begin to notice.

If you are building your own family now, by blood or by choice, you have the opportunity to do things differently. You can pass down love that feels safe instead of conditional. You can show your children what respect looks like, not just what it sounds like. You can create an environment where everyone is allowed to be themselves. That's how generational patterns shift. They change when one person decides to stop repeating what hurt them and start practicing what heals them.

Remember, family is not defined by proximity or shared DNA. It is defined by love, respect, and presence. The people who feel like home are the ones who let you be yourself without fear. Sometimes that's your relatives. Sometimes it's the friends who became family along the way.

You don't have to cut ties with everyone to find peace. You just have to stop tying your peace to everyone. The moment you stop seeking validation from your past, you create space for the kind of family you want in your present.

You can honor your roots without being bound by them. You can love your family while building your own path. And you can carry gratitude for where you came from while still walking freely toward where you are meant to go.

That is what it means to show up more relationally within your family story. Not to rewrite the past, but to live the next chapter with intention, peace, and freedom.

TWENTY

Partnership Without Pressure

Love is one of the most beautiful parts of life, but it is also one of the most misunderstood. Many people spend years chasing the idea of a perfect partner, believing that finding the right person will finally make everything feel complete. Movies, songs, and stories all tell us that real love is about finding our other half. But if you see yourself as half of a person, even the best partner will never make you whole.

A healthy partnership is not built on dependency. It's built on two complete individuals choosing to walk together. It's not about one person fixing the other. It's about both people growing side by side. When you make someone else responsible for your happiness, you hand them a burden they can never carry well. The weight of your peace belongs to you.

Partnerships often begin with excitement and discovery. The early days feel effortless. You want to know everything about the other person. You listen closely. You give freely. You imagine what life could look like together. But over time, reality sets in. Differences appear. Communication gets tested. The version of love that once felt easy now requires intention. This is where many relationships struggle, not because the love is gone, but because people expect connection to stay strong without the same effort that built it.

Pressure begins when love becomes performance. You start trying to anticipate every need, prevent every conflict, and manage every emotion. You try to be perfect because you're afraid imperfection will cost you the relationship. Slowly, love becomes heavy. You stop being present and start performing. That's not partnership. That's survival.

The truth is, love was never meant to be flawless. It was meant to be honest. It's about choosing each other even when it's inconvenient. It's about communicating when silence would be easier. It's about admitting when you're wrong and forgiving when the other person is. Healthy love doesn't remove discomfort. It gives you the tools to face it together.

Partnership without pressure starts with self-awareness. You have to know who you are before you can connect in a healthy way. If you don't understand your own needs and boundaries, you'll expect your partner to guess them. If you don't know what makes you feel safe, you'll make them responsible for creating that safety. When both people enter a relationship aware of their own strengths and flaws, love becomes a collaboration instead of a rescue mission.

Communication is the foundation. Not just talking, but listening. Not just reacting, but understanding. A relationship grows when both people feel free to speak truthfully without fear of punishment. It's not about avoiding arguments but about learning to argue well. It's about remembering that you are on the same side, even when you disagree.

Another part of removing pressure from partnership is allowing space. Space for individuality, space for rest, and space for growth. Constant closeness isn't intimacy. It's dependence. When you can be apart without feeling disconnected, that's trust. Healthy love allows room to breathe. It doesn't need constant reassurance to feel secure.

Partnership also means letting go of comparison. Every relationship is different. What works for one couple might not work for another. Trying to measure your connection against someone else's creates unnecessary pressure. Focus on building something that feels genuine to both of you, not something that looks perfect to others.

In a balanced partnership, both people take responsibility for the energy they bring. They don't expect each other to read minds. They don't punish each other for being human. They understand that mistakes will happen, and when they do, repair matters more than perfection. Love deepens not through the absence of flaws, but through the grace given within them.

Sometimes the hardest part of partnership is learning that love alone is not enough. Without respect, communication, and shared effort, even the strongest feelings fade. Love needs structure. It needs time. It needs attention. It needs two people willing to keep showing up long after the initial spark.

When love is healthy, it doesn't feel like pressure. It feels like peace. It feels like having someone beside you who encourages your growth, not someone who is threatened by it. It feels like being able to be yourself without walking on eggshells. It feels like choosing each other daily, not because you have to, but because you want to.

The best partnerships are not the ones that look perfect from the outside. They are the ones built quietly, with trust, patience, and humility. They are not about who wins or who's right. They are about staying connected when it's hard and celebrating when it's good. They are about creating a rhythm that feels like home to both people.

Love was never meant to complete you. It was meant to complement you. The more whole you are on your own, the more freely you can love without fear. When both people come into a relationship full rather than empty, love stops being a transaction and becomes a gift.

That is partnership without pressure. Two people, grounded in who they are, walking together toward who they are becoming. Not holding each other back. Not trying to fix each other. Just growing, side by side, with grace and honesty.

TWENTY-ONE

Grace in Practice

very relationship, no matter how healthy, will face moments of hurt. Words will be said that should not have been said. Promises will be forgotten. Feelings will be misunderstood. It is part of being human. The question is not whether these moments will happen, but how you respond when they do. That is where grace becomes the difference between relationships that heal and those that harden.

Grace is what allows you to see the person instead of the mistake. It is what lets you pause before reacting and choose understanding over judgment. It doesn't excuse behavior, but it puts compassion before condemnation. Grace is not weakness. It is strength under control. It is choosing to stay soft when life gives you reasons to become hard.

Most people talk about love as if it's a feeling, but love is often proven through grace. Feelings fluctuate. Grace does not. It shows up in how you handle the moments when love feels heavy. It shows up when you forgive even though you're still hurt. It shows up when you try to repair what's been damaged instead of pretending it never happened.

Practicing grace begins with humility. You have to accept that you will fail too. You will say things in frustration that you regret later. You will make assumptions. You will hurt people unintentionally. When you can admit that you are capable of mistakes, it becomes easier to extend understanding when others stumble. Judgment thrives in pride. Grace grows in perspective.

Repair is one of the most powerful expressions of grace. It's not about sweeping conflict under the rug or saying "it's fine" to avoid tension. Repair requires effort. It requires honesty. It begins with the courage to own your part without defending it. "I was wrong. I hurt you. I want to make this right." Those are not easy words to say, but they rebuild trust faster than any explanation ever could.

Apologies mean little without change, and change cannot happen without reflection. Grace invites you to look inward, to ask, "Why did I respond that way? What fear or insecurity was I protecting?" When you understand your triggers, you can approach others with more patience. You stop assuming intention behind every misstep and start focusing on solutions.

Grace also involves boundaries. It is not about letting people walk all over you. Forgiveness without accountability leads to cycles of harm. Grace allows you to forgive someone and still choose distance if necessary. You can wish someone well without continuing a relationship that repeatedly hurts you. True grace includes wisdom. It does not ignore truth for the sake of comfort.

Extending grace does not mean you allow disrespect. It means you refuse to let bitterness define you. You can forgive someone and still hold them accountable. You can love someone and still protect yourself. The balance of grace and truth is what creates real peace.

Receiving grace is often harder than giving it. Many people are comfortable offering forgiveness but uncomfortable being forgiven. They struggle to accept that others can see their flaws and still love them. But relationships require both. If you want to experience closeness, you have to allow yourself to be human in front of others. You have to accept that love can exist even after you fall short.

Grace has a quiet way of healing what pride destroys. It softens anger. It rebuilds safety. It allows connection to recover after pain. The relationships that last are not the ones without conflict. They are the ones where grace shows up faster than blame.

To live with grace means to let go of the need to always be right. It means to value peace over winning. It means to treat people with gentleness even when you could choose judgment. Grace does not erase boundaries. It reinforces them with kindness. It keeps your heart open without leaving it unguarded.

If you want to see what grace looks like in action, notice the small moments. It's the text that says, "I'm sorry for how I spoke earlier." It's the friend who checks in after a fight. It's the partner who chooses patience instead of defensiveness. It's the quiet forgiveness that happens without fanfare. Grace rarely announces itself, but it changes everything it touches.

You don't need to be perfect to live with grace. You only need to remember that everyone, including you, is doing the best they can with what they know. Grace gives people space to grow while still holding them accountable to truth. It turns conflict into connection and mistakes into lessons.

Grace is love that refuses to quit. It's patience in practice. It's forgiveness without forgetting the wisdom that came with the wound. It's the bridge that carries relationships through the storms they cannot avoid.

When you lead with grace, people feel safe enough to be real. And where people can be real, love can finally breathe.

TWENTY-TWO

When Love and Loyalty Collide

There is an old story about a farmer who owned two oxen. For years they worked side by side, pulling the same plow through the same soil. The farmer depended on them. He knew their rhythm, their strength, their steps. One day, after a heavy storm, one ox slipped and injured its leg. The farmer did everything he could to heal it. He gave it rest, wrapped the wound, adjusted the harness so it could still walk. But no matter how much he tried, the injured ox couldn't keep up.

Still, the farmer couldn't bring himself to separate them. He loved them both. So he kept them tied together, hoping that the strong one could carry the load for both. Each day he pulled harder, sweating through the fields, forcing the plow forward. The work that used to take an afternoon now took him until dusk. By the end of the season, neither ox had the strength they once had. The field suffered too. Crops grew in patches, uneven and thin.

One morning, as he looked over his land, the farmer finally understood what he'd done. He had spent the entire season fighting against what was already true. He had used all his effort trying to return things to how they used to be, instead of accepting how they were.

So he untied the rope. He led the injured ox to a shaded pasture where it could rest, then returned to the field with the one still strong enough to pull. The work was quieter, slower, and lonelier, but it was honest. For the first time in months, the field began to thrive again.

The story isn't about oxen. It's about us.

So many people live their lives like that farmer. They keep pouring time, energy, and emotion into something that has already changed. A friendship that no longer feels safe, a partner who has stopped showing up, a parent they've been trying to please for decades. Out of love, loyalty, or fear, they refuse to see what is right in front of them. They think if they just try harder, they can fix it, heal it, save it. But there's a difference between effort and attachment.

Sometimes the hardest part of love is accepting reality.

You can spend years trying to bring something back to life that simply isn't meant to be carried anymore. You can tie yourself to the version of someone who no longer exists, holding on to memories instead of seeing the person they've become. And the more you fight the truth, the heavier the plow becomes.

Loyalty tells you to keep pulling. Love, in its truest form, whispers that it's time to let go.

When love and loyalty collide, the temptation is to keep investing, to keep trying to make things work out the way you imagined. You tell yourself that quitting means failure, that walking away means you never cared enough. But often, staying too long in something that no longer fits is what actually breaks you.

I once worked with someone who stayed in a relationship years past its health. Every conversation ended in apology. Every day felt like walking on glass. When I asked why she didn't leave, she said, "Because I promised I'd never give up." What she didn't see was that she had already given up something far more important. Herself.

That's what happens when loyalty loses direction. It turns into sacrifice. You start confusing devotion with endurance. You keep investing in a version of love that only exists in your memory. You keep hoping for change instead of facing the truth that maybe it's not supposed to change.

The farmer didn't fail because he loved his oxen. He failed because he refused to accept that love alone couldn't undo reality. He could have spent his time tending the rest of his field, caring for the animals that were still strong, or preparing for the next season. Instead, he exhausted himself trying to force something broken to behave as if it were whole.

We do the same thing. We stay in relationships that no longer bring peace. We defend people who keep crossing boundaries. We cling to roles or identities that used to define us. All because we think holding on makes us strong. But true strength is knowing when to redirect your effort.

Acceptance is not weakness. It's wisdom. It's recognizing that your energy is sacred and limited, and that spending it trying to change what refuses to change only empties you. Acceptance doesn't mean you stop caring. It means you care differently. It means you release what cannot be restored so you can nurture what still can.

There's a moment in every life where you have to ask yourself, "Is my loyalty to this person, or to the truth?"

If your loyalty to a relationship costs you your peace, your joy, or your self-respect, it's no longer loyalty. It's fear. And fear will always keep you tied to what's already over.

I've seen people waste years in this tug-of-war with reality. Convincing themselves that staying proves love, when all it proves is resistance. The longer you fight the truth, the more damage you do to yourself and the people you're trying to save.

But something powerful happens the moment you stop fighting. The moment you stop asking, "How can I fix this?" and start asking, "What is this trying to teach me?" That's when peace begins to return.

You may not like the answer, but you'll feel lighter for hearing it.

When the farmer finally accepted what was real, his world didn't fall apart. It got quieter, clearer, simpler. He didn't stop caring for the ox he loved. He just stopped asking it to do what it couldn't do anymore. He redirected his energy toward what could still grow. And in that acceptance, life began to move again.

That's what letting go really is. Not rejection, not apathy, but alignment. It's acknowledging that the story has changed, and that fighting it only keeps you stuck in the last chapter.

So if you find yourself in a relationship, friendship, or season of life that feels like pulling a plow that will not move, take a breath. Look at where your energy is going. Ask yourself if you're trying to revive what has already ended. Ask yourself if you're chasing peace or forcing it.

You are allowed to stop trying to make things what they used to be. You are allowed to love someone and still accept that they're not meant to go where you're going next. You are allowed to free yourself without guilt.

The farmer didn't fail by letting go. He failed by waiting so long to do it.

When love and loyalty collide, let truth be your compass. Love doesn't always mean holding tighter. Sometimes it means loosening your grip, accepting what is, and trusting that your energy is better spent tending what can still grow.

Because some things are meant to be carried. Others are meant to be released. And learning the difference is where peace begins.

TWENTY-THREE

In Good Times and Bad

In the last chapter, I told you the story of the farmer and his two oxen — how one grew too weak to pull and how the farmer finally accepted that reality. But it's important to remember something about that story. The ox was not lazy. It was not distracted, stubborn, or unwilling. It was old, tired, and truly unable to keep going. The farmer didn't give up because the work got hard. He let go because the truth had become unchangeable.

That distinction matters.

Too many people hear stories like that and use them as a reason to quit the moment things stop feeling easy. They confuse discomfort with dysfunction. They confuse struggle with finality. The truth is, sometimes the relationship doesn't need to be released. It needs to be repaired.

There is a difference between something that is broken beyond repair and something that is simply asking to be strengthened.

Every commitment worth keeping will go through storms. Every promise will be tested. When you said you would love in good times and in bad, this is what "bad" looks like. It's not betrayal or disaster. Sometimes it's boredom. Sometimes it's frustration. Sometimes it's two people trying to grow in different directions without realizing that they can still choose each other through it.

We live in a world that glorifies newness and convenience. If something breaks, we replace it. If someone disappoints us, we block them. If the spark fades, we assume the love is gone. But lasting connection was never meant to be disposable. It's meant to be refined through challenge.

You can't build depth without friction. You can't learn faithfulness without resistance.

There was a couple I once knew who had been married for more than forty years. When I asked them how they made it last, the husband said something I'll never forget. "We didn't fall in love and stay there," he said. "We fell in love and built a life. There's a difference."

He told me about years when money was tight, when they barely spoke, when both felt misunderstood. But they made a choice — to stay, to talk, to forgive. Not because it was easy, but because it mattered. "Love is a feeling," he said, "but loyalty is a decision."

That's what people often forget. Feelings are seasonal. They come and go like weather. Commitment is the anchor that holds through it.

There will be seasons when you don't feel inspired by your partner, your friend, or even your own family. You will question why you keep showing up. You will wonder whether it's worth it. Those moments don't mean you're in the wrong place. They mean you're human. Every long relationship has chapters that feel dull or distant. Those chapters are where love matures.

In those seasons, you don't walk away. You lean in. You ask questions. You look for the truth beneath the fatigue. You remind yourself why you chose this person, this family, this friend in the first place.

If the ox in the last story had simply been stubborn or distracted, the farmer would have trained it, not released it. That's what we are called to do in relationships that still have life left in them. We work with patience. We repair with humility. We communicate instead of assume. We stop waiting for the feeling to return and start rebuilding it.

Effort doesn't mean suffering endlessly. It means giving honesty a chance to work before deciding it cannot.

I have seen people throw away good relationships because they expected perpetual excitement. They didn't understand that comfort can be sacred too. The quiet seasons, the ordinary days, the routine moments. These are not signs of decline. They are the soil where loyalty grows.

Love, at its core, is not about constant passion. It's about choosing care when you're tired, respect when you're frustrated, and grace when you don't feel like giving it. It's about remembering that the same person who annoys you today might be the one holding your hand through something harder tomorrow.

None of us are easy to love all the time. We are all, in some way, that injured ox from the last story — slow, tired, imperfect, needing patience. The question is whether we can show each other that kind of grace.

Of course, not every relationship is meant to last forever. Some truly do reach the end of their road, and letting go becomes the most loving thing to do. But most of the time, the problem isn't that the love has died. It's that we've stopped tending to it.

Every connection requires maintenance. It requires effort that isn't glamorous. The kind that looks like showing up to uncomfortable conversations, apologizing first, forgiving second, and trying again the next morning. It's the small, ordinary work that no one applauds but that holds everything together.

When you stand before someone and make a promise — in friendship, marriage, or family — that promise isn't just for the easy parts. It's a vow to stay steady through the messy, confusing, exhausting parts too.

Good times test your gratitude. Bad times test your character.

When life feels easy, it's natural to believe love is strong. But real strength shows in the moments that stretch you thin. It's in the nights you stay even when everything in you wants to leave. It's in the mornings when you wake up and decide to try again even though you're still hurt.

Staying doesn't mean tolerating harm. It means recognizing that growth often feels like discomfort. It means knowing that repair is slower than destruction, but always more worthwhile.

If you're in a season that feels heavy, don't assume it's the end. Ask whether you've truly done the work to restore it. Have you communicated honestly? Have you listened with humility? Have you softened your heart enough to give healing a chance?

Sometimes love is saved not by grand gestures, but by small moments of grace, a hand on the shoulder, a shared laugh after tension, a willingness to see the best in someone even when they're at their worst.

The promise you made, whether spoken or unspoken, wasn't to stay only when it feels good. It was to keep showing up, learning, forgiving, and growing, in good times and in bad.

The difference between the relationships that last and the ones that fade isn't luck. It's perseverance. It's two people who decide that the story isn't over yet, even when it feels hard to turn the next page.

The farmer learned when it was time to release what could no longer work. But before you make that same choice, make sure you've done what he did first, every possible effort to nurture what still can.

Love is built in the tension between truth and loyalty. The art is knowing when to hold on and when to let go.

In good times, love feels effortless. In bad times, it becomes a discipline. But both seasons have purpose. Both reveal who we are when comfort is gone and character takes over.

So stay when staying builds you. Work when work can heal you. And when the time for letting go does come, let it be after every act of faithfulness has already been tried.

Because love, real love, is not proven in how easy it is to begin. It's proven in how faithfully we choose to continue.

TWENTY-FOUR

Seeing Clearly in the Middle

When relationships get hard, perspective is usually the first thing to disappear. In the heat of it, everything feels louder. Every silence feels heavier. Every word feels sharper than it was meant to be. It's in that fog that most people make their worst decisions — walking away from what could have been repaired, or staying tied to what has already drained them dry.

That's why before you can know what to do, you have to learn how to see clearly.

The truth is that clarity rarely shows up when things are peaceful. It's born in tension. You find out who you are and who someone else is when the connection gets strained. But to read those moments accurately, you have to stay steady enough not to lose yourself in them.

Most people don't fail at relationships because they don't care. They fail because they get swallowed by the storm. Their emotions get louder than their values. Their fear starts calling the shots.

When love hurts, our first instinct is to ask, "What did I do wrong?" But not every struggle is your fault, and not every change means you failed. Sometimes what you're feeling isn't a sign of brokenness; it's a sign of growth. The key is to learn how to tell the difference.

There are three questions that bring almost any situation into focus:

1. Am I acting from love or from fear? Fear makes you shrink, overthink, and try to control what you can't. It makes you chase after someone who has already pulled away or apologize for things that weren't yours to fix. Love, on the other hand, doesn't panic. It doesn't have to prove itself. It steadies you. When your choices are rooted in love, they're usually calm, even when they hurt.

2. Is this connection helping me grow or keeping me small? Healthy relationships challenge you, but they don't erase you. They make you more honest, more grounded, more alive. Unhealthy ones make you question your worth. You start walking on eggshells, silencing yourself to keep the peace. If you have to become smaller to stay connected, that's not love. That's survival.

3. Am I carrying my share or carrying both sides? Every relationship requires effort. But there's a difference between contributing and carrying. When you carry, you take on responsibility for someone else's healing, emotions, or growth. You start managing their half and yours. It will always feel noble in the moment, but it quietly burns you out. The truth is, you can support someone, but you can't walk their path for them.

When you start to see those patterns clearly, guilt begins to fade. You realize that you don't have to label someone as a villain or yourself as a failure. Sometimes two good people are just no longer growing in the same direction. Sometimes love is real, but alignment is gone.

Clarity doesn't mean you stop caring. It just means you stop confusing compassion with control.

If you grew up in chaos, you probably learned early to read every mood, to keep everyone calm, to fix what was never yours to fix. That survival skill becomes a pattern in adulthood. You attach by managing. You mistake stability for safety. You pour into others so they won't leave. But healing that pattern means realizing that your worth isn't tied to how well you maintain peace. You are allowed to exist without always being the one who repairs everything.

Seeing clearly starts when you stop taking total responsibility for everyone else's happiness.

I once spoke with a woman who said, "Every relationship I've had ends the same way. I give everything, and they still leave." As we talked, she realized that her giving was never balanced. She gave to earn love, not to share it. Every act of care came with quiet fear attached — fear of being unneeded, unwanted, replaceable. She wasn't loving freely. She was negotiating safety.

Once she saw that, she stopped blaming herself for being "too much" and started asking better questions. Instead of, "Why do people leave me?" she asked, "Why do I only feel safe when I'm needed?" That shift changed everything.

You can't see truth when you're caught in defense. You have to slow down long enough to notice what's yours and what isn't.

When things feel off in a relationship, pause before you act. Ask yourself:

- What part of this is actually mine to own?

- What part belongs to them?

- What am I feeling right now — fear, anger, disappointment, grief? Naming it separates the emotion from the identity. It lets you respond with wisdom instead of reaction.

When you see clearly, you stop internalizing every problem as proof of your inadequacy. You begin to realize that sometimes people pull away not because you failed, but because they are lost in their own pain. Sometimes they change because life changed them, not because you weren't enough.

You can love someone deeply and still acknowledge that their healing is not your assignment. You can want reconciliation and still choose boundaries. You can stay soft without staying stuck.

Clarity doesn't remove pain. It removes distortion. It lets you see what's really happening, not what fear tells you is happening.

If you feel constantly anxious in a relationship, ask whether that anxiety comes from what's real or from what's remembered. Many of us aren't reacting to the person in front of us. We're reacting to every time we've ever felt unseen. When old wounds get triggered, we stop seeing the present clearly. The way back is to pause before assuming. Breathe before deciding. Respond from peace, not panic.

Seeing clearly doesn't always change the relationship, but it always changes you. You start speaking with more honesty. You stop apologizing for your needs. You stop confusing boundaries with rejection. You stop chasing people who only meet you halfway.

And perhaps most importantly, you stop making yourself the project.

Every person who wants to grow in love has to face this truth: you can't do both sides of the work. You can only show up as the healthiest version of yourself and invite others to meet you there. Some will. Some won't. That's not a measure of your worth. That's just reality.

When you see that clearly, you begin to love differently. Not harder, but wiser. You stop mistaking intensity for intimacy. You stop assuming that effort will always equal outcome. You start valuing peace over proving yourself.

That's how you stay balanced when everything feels amplified — by knowing what's yours to hold and what isn't.

So before you decide what a relationship means, take a step back. Quiet the noise. Feel your feet on the ground. Ask for truth, not comfort.

And remember this: you cannot lose yourself trying to save something that is meant to teach you.

Clarity will show you the difference.

TWENTY-FIVE

Grace and Space

After doing all this work, it's easy to start seeing every relationship through a microscope. You begin to notice every imbalance, every silence, every small misstep. What once felt normal now stands out. And for a while, that can make you feel like you're surrounded by brokenness. Like everything needs fixing.

But here's the truth. Growth will always make the world look uneven at first. You aren't seeing more problems. You're just seeing with clearer eyes.

That clarity is a gift, but it can also be a trap if you forget what the purpose of it was. This work was never about finding perfect people or flawless relationships. It was about learning to show up as your whole self without losing peace.

Once you've learned to see differently, the next step is to love differently. That's where grace and space come in.

Grace is what keeps clarity from turning into criticism. Space is what keeps love from turning into control.

Grace reminds you that everyone, including you, is still learning. It softens the edge of judgment and makes room for people to grow at their own pace. It allows you to hold someone accountable without holding them hostage to who they used to be.

Space reminds you that relationships can breathe. That connection isn't meant to be constant pressure. That sometimes the healthiest thing you can do for someone is to step back enough for them to rise on their own.

Together, grace and space form the foundation of mature love.

You can have all the boundaries in the world, but without grace, they turn into walls. You can have all the compassion in the world, but without space, it turns into suffocation. Balance is where love lives.

There will be people in your life who are still figuring themselves out. People who can't yet meet you where you are. Your work is not to shrink back to meet them. It's to stay steady and kind while giving them room to catch up.

You can't make anyone grow faster than they're ready for. But you can model what healthy looks like. You can be the calm in the room instead of the storm.

That's what it means to show up with grace. It means choosing patience over pride. It means speaking truth without anger. It means offering forgiveness without forgetting what you've learned.

And when you add space to that grace, love becomes sustainable. You stop needing constant reassurance. You stop measuring closeness by proximity. You start understanding that love is sometimes silent, and silence doesn't always mean distance.

The most peaceful relationships aren't the ones that avoid tension. They're the ones that know how to move through it without losing connection.

If there's anything this journey has taught, it's that showing up relationally begins and ends with you. The relationship you have with yourself sets the tone for every other one. When you are grounded, you stop reacting to every mood around you. When you are at peace, you become the safe place others can lean on.

That's the real power of doing this work. You become the kind of person who doesn't need to fix people to love them. You can sit with them in their process. You can give them grace to grow and space to breathe, while still protecting your own peace.

Some people will meet you there. Some won't. Both are okay.

The goal was never to control outcomes. The goal was to become someone who shows up honestly, loves freely, and lets life unfold without losing themselves in the process.

So if you take nothing else from this book, take this. You do not have to carry the weight of every relationship. You just have to carry yourself well within them.

That is how you keep showing up more. With grace, with space, and with peace that cannot be taken from you.

TWENTY-SIX

The Flywheel of Connection

Every healthy relationship begins with awareness, grows through honesty, and endures through grace. When those pieces work together, they create something powerful. Connection stops being something you chase and becomes something you live. It becomes a rhythm, a steady cycle that feeds itself. That is the flywheel of connection.

A flywheel is a simple mechanism that stores energy through movement. The more it turns, the more momentum it builds. Relationships work the same way. Each time you show up with honesty, each time you choose to listen instead of defend, each time you forgive instead of withdraw, you add energy to the connection. Over time, that effort builds something strong enough to keep moving even when life gets heavy.

The hardest part is starting. In the beginning, it takes effort to be mindful of your tone, to communicate clearly, to stay calm during conflict. It takes work to set boundaries, to listen without interrupting, to express needs without fear. But once those things become habits, they start to sustain each other. Healthy patterns reinforce themselves just like unhealthy ones do. The difference is that one drains you while the other restores you.

When you have practiced showing up for yourself, you bring a different kind of presence to others. You stop needing people to complete you because you already feel whole. You stop needing to prove your worth because you already know it. You begin to approach relationships with peace instead of pressure. That inner stability becomes the foundation for every other form of connection.

As you continue to grow, you will notice how interconnected everything becomes. Your ability to listen improves because you feel secure enough not to take things personally. Your boundaries strengthen because you no longer confuse guilt with love. Your relationships deepen because you no longer hide behind performance. Every area of growth feeds the next. That is the flywheel in motion.

There will still be challenges. Life will always bring seasons of distance, misunderstanding, and change. But when the flywheel is turning, those moments do not derail you. They become part of the process. You know how to communicate through conflict, how to repair with grace, how to rest without disconnecting. You have practiced the tools that keep connection alive.

The beauty of relational growth is that it multiplies. When you show up differently, others start to respond differently. Your calm invites calm. Your honesty encourages honesty. Your grace makes people feel safe enough to admit when they are wrong. Over time, this energy spreads. It changes the tone of your friendships, your family, your partnerships, even your work environment. One healthy relationship creates the model for others to follow.

You will still make mistakes. You will still have moments of frustration and fear. But the difference is that you will not stay stuck in them. You will know how to return to center, how to apologize, how to rebuild. The work never ends, but it gets easier. Each choice builds momentum. Each moment of awareness keeps the wheel turning.

This is what it means to show up more relationally. It's not about perfection. It's about consistency. It's about living in a way that keeps connection alive through intention and humility. It's about practicing what you've learned, even when no one else notices.

When you choose to live this way, you create relationships that feel steady, honest, and peaceful. You stop chasing love and start cultivating it. You stop fearing loss and start trusting the process. You begin to see that connection is not something you find once and hold forever. It's something you build every day, one act of awareness at a time.

The flywheel of connection keeps turning as long as you keep showing up. Each time you practice what you've learned, you make it easier to do again. Each moment of grace creates space for more love. Each step toward honesty invites deeper trust.

That is how relationships grow strong enough to last. Not through luck or perfection, but through steady movement. Through showing up, again and again, with truth, kindness, and courage.

When you live this way, connection becomes less about effort and more about alignment. You find peace not because everyone around you changes, but because you have. You've learned that love is built, not found. You've learned that growth is constant. You've learned that grace is never wasted.

Keep the flywheel turning. Keep showing up. Keep choosing connection over control, presence over performance, and truth over comfort. Because when you do, love will not just visit your life. It will stay.

TWENTY-SEVEN

Closing Note

If you've made it this far, take a breath and let that mean something.

Reading a book about relationships is one thing. Living it is another. It takes humility to look at your own patterns. It takes courage to admit where you've been hurt or where you've hurt others. It takes strength to keep showing up when it would be easier to shut down. So pause for a moment and give yourself credit. You didn't just read this book. You walked through it.

What I hope you've seen along the way is that relationships aren't just about connection with others. They are about reflection, awareness, and growth. Every relationship — with yourself, your friends, your family, your partner — offers a chance to become more grounded, more patient, more present. Even the painful ones leave behind wisdom if you're willing to look for it.

The goal isn't to get it perfect. The goal is to stay engaged. You will still make mistakes. You will still misunderstand people. You will still have moments where you overgive, overthink, or overreact. That's okay. The work of showing up more relationally isn't about never falling short. It's about learning how to return faster each time you do.

There is a quiet kind of peace that comes when you stop chasing flawless relationships and start building honest ones. When you stop trying to be everything to everyone and start being present with the few who matter most. When you learn that connection isn't about fixing, proving, or earning. It's about being fully human, together.

If this book has reminded you of something you lost, I hope it also reminded you that you can rebuild. If it made you aware of a pattern, I hope it gave you grace instead of shame. If it opened your eyes to how much love you already have, I hope it inspires you to keep nurturing it.

Every person you love — including you — deserves relationships that feel safe, truthful, and alive. You don't have to do it all at once. Just start where you are. One honest conversation. One clear boundary. One moment of forgiveness. Over time, those small choices change everything.

Keep showing up for yourself. Keep showing up for others. Keep tending to the connections that bring light into your life. Because when you do, you'll find that love isn't a mystery to solve. It's a rhythm to live by.

And that rhythm, once it starts, has the power to change everything.

TWENTY-EIGHT

Relationship Index

Relationships are the mirror through which we learn who we are. Every connection in your life tells you something about yourself, whether it's through comfort, tension, or growth. This section is here to help you see those patterns clearly.

The goal is not to label people or decide who is right or wrong. It's to understand *how* you relate. Most of us fall into familiar patterns without realizing it. Some feel nurturing. Some feel draining. Some start healthy and slowly drift off balance. Once you can name the pattern, you can change it.

Each dynamic in this index describes a common pattern that can show up in any type of relationship. These are not fixed roles. They are just reflections of the ways we cope, protect, and connect. You might see yourself on one side in one relationship and the opposite side in another. That is normal.

The point is to recognize what happens so you can grow through it.

Here's how to use this section:

- **Find the pattern that fits.** Read through the titles and notice which ones sound familiar. You'll know when one hits home.

- **Look at both sides.** Each entry shows how the dynamic plays out for both people. This helps you see your part and theirs without blame.

- **Notice the signs.** Each pattern includes what it looks like when it's healthy and when it's not.

- **Use the guidance.** Each section ends with simple ways to shift the relationship toward balance. Try one idea at a time. Small changes create lasting growth.

This is not a test of whether you're doing relationships "right." It's a guide to help you see them clearly. When you understand the role you play, you gain the power to show up differently.

Take your time. Reflect honestly. You might find that what feels like a problem is just an old pattern asking to be healed.

When you see your relationships for what they are, not what you wish they were, you finally get to choose what happens next.

***

The Parent–Child Dynamic

The parent–child dynamic happens when one person takes on the role of caretaker or decision-maker while the other becomes dependent or passive. It doesn't matter if you're friends, partners, or coworkers. This can happen anywhere. One person leads, gives advice, and keeps everything in order. The other starts to rely on them, letting them decide, fix, or plan most things.

At first, it can feel safe. The "parent" feels useful and needed. The "child" feels cared for and protected. But over time, this pattern gets heavy for both sides.

When you are the "parent" in the relationship: You might be the one who always plans, fixes, or worries. You check in first, smooth over conflict, and take care of details because you want things to work. You might even say things like, "If I don't do it, it won't get done." Deep down, you don't mean to control anyone. You just want to help. But sometimes helping turns into managing, and managing can turn into resentment.

You may start to feel like you're carrying the whole relationship while the other person coasts. You might feel unseen for how much effort you put in. But what you really are is tired.

When you are the "child" in the relationship: You might notice that the other person often takes the lead, so you let them. You might tell yourself, "They're better at this than I am," or "I don't want to mess it up." Over time, you stop speaking up or making choices because it feels easier to just follow along.

At first, being cared for feels nice. But eventually, it can make you feel small or dependent. You may even start to rebel or pull away, not because you don't care, but because you want to breathe.

When this dynamic is unhealthy: The "parent" becomes tired and frustrated. The "child" feels trapped or guilty. The relationship starts to feel unbalanced. The "parent" may start to use guilt to get appreciation. The "child" may shut down or avoid the "parent" completely. Both people end up feeling misunderstood and lonely.

When it's healthy: Healthy care doesn't mean control, and support doesn't mean dependence. A balanced version of this relationship still has love and safety, but also respect and space. Both people take responsibility for themselves. The "parent" learns to trust others to handle things. The "child" learns to trust themselves.

When this dynamic is healthy, advice turns into conversation. Decisions are shared. Effort is mutual. You both get to relax.

How to make it healthier: If you notice yourself acting like the "parent," try to step back. You don't have to fix everything. Ask questions instead of giving instructions. Say things like, "What do you think would work best?" or "How can I support you?" This shows trust and builds confidence.

If you notice yourself acting like the "child," start taking small steps toward independence. Make your own choices, even if they're not perfect. When someone offers to take over, say, "I've got this, but thank you." Every time you take ownership, the balance shifts a little closer to healthy.

If you both see this pattern happening, talk about it. Say what you need without blame. The "parent" might say, "I realize I've been taking over too much, and I want to stop." The "child" might say, "I want to take on more responsibility because I don't want you to feel alone in this."

When both people understand their part, the whole relationship feels lighter. You stop playing roles and start being real people again. You learn to care *with* each other, not *for* each other.

That's what a healthy relationship looks like — not one person leading and the other following, but two people walking side by side.

The Hero–Victim Dynamic

The hero–victim dynamic happens when one person is always trying to save the other. One becomes the hero, the other becomes the victim. The hero wants to fix things. The victim wants to be saved. At first, it might look like love or loyalty, but after a while, it starts to wear both people out.

When you are the hero: You want to help. You feel calm when you can make things better. You listen, you advise, you give and give. You may even tell yourself that if you don't help, no one else will. It feels good to be needed, and it feels awful when someone you care about struggles.

But over time, this can become a trap. You start carrying other people's pain like it is your job to fix it. When they do not take your advice, you feel frustrated. When they get better, you feel relieved. When they don't, you feel like you failed.

You may not notice it, but being the hero keeps you distracted from your own pain. It feels easier to fix others than to face your own hard stuff.

When you are the victim: You might find comfort in having someone always ready to help. It feels nice to be cared for. But over time, you may start believing you can't handle things on your own. You might think you are broken, or that you always need saving.

When help is always offered, it is easy to stop trying. It is also easy to feel guilty or defensive, because deep down you know you want to stand on your own two feet, but you do not know how.

When this dynamic is unhealthy: Both people end up exhausted. The hero feels unappreciated. The victim feels controlled. The relationship becomes about fixing problems instead of growing together. The hero starts to resent the weight they carry. The victim starts to resent being seen as a project.

No one wins.

When it is healthy: Healthy help is support, not rescue. The hero learns to offer encouragement without taking over. The victim learns to ask for help without giving up their power. Both people understand that love does not mean doing everything for each other. It means walking beside each other while both take responsibility for their own choices.

In a healthy version of this dynamic, the hero listens more and fixes less. The victim takes more small steps on their own. There is honesty, respect, and space for both people to grow.

How to make it healthier: If you notice you often play the hero, try to pause before you jump in. Instead of saying, "Let me do that for you," try saying, "How can I support you while you do this?" Let people struggle a little. That is how they build strength.

If you see yourself as the victim, remind yourself that you are not helpless. You might need help sometimes, but you are still capable. Take one small action on your own, even if it feels scary. Prove to yourself that you can handle more than you thought.

And if both people notice this pattern, talk about it. The hero can say, "I realize I keep trying to fix everything, and I don't want to take your power away." The victim can say, "I appreciate your help, but I want to learn to do more myself."

Healthy love builds confidence in both directions. It doesn't make one person feel powerful and the other small.

The goal is not to stop helping each other. It is to help in a way that leaves both people stronger when it is done.

The Mirror Dynamic

The mirror dynamic happens when someone in your life reflects parts of you that you have not fully faced yet. This can be a partner, a friend, a parent, a sibling, or a coworker. The connection often feels intense because this person brings up both your best and your hardest parts. Sometimes you feel close to them. Sometimes you feel irritated by them. Both are clues.

You might catch yourself saying, "They always do this and it drives me crazy." Then later you realize you do a version of the very same thing. Maybe they interrupt. Maybe they withdraw. Maybe they get loud. Maybe they get quiet. Whatever it is, it touches a nerve in you. That nerve is the mirror.

When you are the one being reflected: You feel triggered by behavior that seems small from the outside. You may overreact. You may get sarcastic or go cold. You focus on what they are doing wrong. Underneath that anger is usually an old story. A time you felt unheard. A time you felt pushed aside. The mirror shows where you still hurt or where you still hide.

When you are the mirror for someone else: You may notice someone reacts strongly to you. You do not think you did anything that serious. They seem to take things the wrong way. They might accuse. They might withdraw. Often, they are not responding to this moment. They are responding to a pattern from their past that your behavior touched. It helps not to take it personally.

When this dynamic is unhealthy: You both blame. You repeat the same argument. You talk about the details instead of the pattern. You try to win the moment instead of understanding the mirror. The relationship starts to feel like a loop. No one feels seen. No one feels safe.

When it is healthy: You notice the trigger and get curious. You can say, "That hit me harder than it should have. I want to understand why." You slow down. You breathe. You ask yourself, "Where have I felt this before?" You start separating the present from the past. You take ownership of your reaction instead of turning it into an accusation.

How to make it healthier: If you feel triggered, pause. Name the feeling with simple words. Angry. Sad. Afraid. Ashamed. Then ask what story sits under that feeling. Do not rush. Let the truth come up. Share it without blame. Say, "When this happens, I feel like I do not matter." That is very different from, "You never care."

If someone is projecting onto you, keep boundaries and use gentle clarity. Say, "I hear that this feels big. That was not my intent. I want to understand." Do not argue every point. Do not match their volume. Calm truth helps the mirror do its work.

The mirror is a gift when you let it be. It can help you grow faster than any book or class. It will not always feel comfortable. But it will always point you toward the part of you that needs care.

People do not only show you who they are. They also show you who you are still becoming. When you learn to see that, the mirror stops feeling like an enemy. It becomes your teacher. And your relationships get lighter, kinder, and more honest.

The Transactional Dynamic

The transactional dynamic shows up when a relationship runs on exchange instead of care. It sounds like fairness. It looks efficient. It often starts with good intentions. You give. I give. We both keep things even. Over time, though, giving turns into keeping score. Love starts to feel like a trade. Warmth fades.

When you are the giver: You do a lot. You plan, remember dates, pick up the slack, and show up first. You tell yourself you are kind. You are. But you also hope the other person will match your effort. When they do not, you feel invisible. You think, "After all I do, really?"

When you are the taker: You may not notice the effort that holds things together. You think, "They like doing it." You are not trying to use anyone. You simply assume the machine will keep running. Then the energy shifts. They pull back. You feel confusion and sometimes guilt.

When this dynamic is unhealthy: Every gesture becomes a ledger entry. The giver feels unappreciated and tense. The taker feels managed and judged. Gratitude disappears. Obligation takes over. People start saying yes when they mean no. Resentment grows in quiet places.

When it is healthy: There is still giving and receiving, but the energy is different. Giving is a choice, not a currency. Receiving comes with thanks, not with entitlement. Balance is measured over time, not moment by moment. Both people feel free to say yes or no.

How to make it healthier: If you are the giver, check your motive before you act. Ask, "Am I doing this because I want to, or because I am afraid not to?" If it is fear, pause. Either give freely or do not give at all. If you want something, ask for it directly. Do not expect unspoken debts to be repaid.

If you are the taker, look for invisible labor. Who schedules, reminds, cleans up, or carries the emotional work? Say thank you. Then ask, "What can I take off your plate this week?" Do the task without being asked twice. Small effort restores trust fast.

If both of you see this pattern, put words to it. Say, "I want our giving to feel like joy, not pressure." Agree to fewer unspoken expectations. Agree to clearer asks and cleaner no's. Make appreciation normal. It changes the air in the room.

The goal is not perfect fairness. The goal is a warm heart and a clear yes. When generosity replaces transaction, relationships feel alive again. People lean in. Resentment fades. Love starts to sound like, "I wanted to," not, "I had to."

The Competitor Dynamic

The competitor dynamic happens when comparison replaces connection. It can show up between friends, partners, siblings, or coworkers. At first it can feel motivating. You push each other. You try new things. You grow. But slowly, the mood shifts. Wins feel like threats. Losses feel like shame. The room gets tight.

When you are the competitor: You pay attention to who did what. You notice their success and feel a pinch. You want to be happy for them, but you also feel behind. You might make small jokes, hedge your compliments, or rush to share your own win. You are not trying to be cruel. You are trying to not feel small.

Often this pattern began long ago. Maybe love felt tied to achievement. Maybe attention only came when you excelled. Now your nervous system treats every scoreboard like a verdict. It is hard to relax when you believe your worth is on the line.

When you are on the receiving end of competition: You share good news and feel the air change. You sense distance. You stop sharing as much to avoid tension. You hold back joy. That holding back slowly starves the friendship or partnership. It becomes safer to be average than to be honest.

When this dynamic is unhealthy: Trust drops. People hide struggles. People hide success. Conversations turn into highlight reels or quiet withdrawal. You stop cheering for each other. You start keeping score. In the end, both feel alone.

When it is healthy: Competition becomes inspiration. Your win lifts me. My win lifts you. We can both be strong in our own lanes. We can ask for help without shame and give it without pride. We can admire without comparing.

How to make it healthier: Name it gently. Say, "I value us more than any scoreboard. I want to celebrate each other without pressure." Then prove it with action. Give clean praise. "You did great." Stop there. No comparison. No pivot. Let joy be simple.

Share your real story. Not just wins. Not just losses. Tell the truth about the middle. When honesty walks in, competition loses its teeth. It is hard to envy someone you also understand.

Create shared goals. Build something together. Train together. Learn together. Turn rivalry into teamwork on purpose. When you face the same direction, you stop facing off.

Your worth is not a race. Neither is love. The more you practice that truth, the easier it gets to celebrate others and still feel solid in yourself. That is how the competitor dynamic becomes fuel for growth instead of friction that wears you down.

The Ghost–Chaser Dynamic

The ghost–chaser dynamic happens when one person pulls away and the other keeps chasing after them. It is a push and pull that leaves both people feeling frustrated and unseen. The ghost needs space. The chaser needs closeness. The harder one runs, the harder the other tries to catch up.

This pattern can appear in any relationship. It might be romantic, but it can also show up between friends, family members, or coworkers. At first, it may even look exciting. The ghost feels powerful and free. The chaser feels hopeful and determined. But underneath, both are scared of the same thing: rejection.

When you are the ghost: You might pull away when things get emotional or uncertain. You may not mean to hurt anyone. You just need time to think or breathe. When things start to feel too close or too intense, you disappear for a bit. You tell yourself you will come back when you are ready.

But every time you leave without explanation, the other person feels more anxious. They start to wonder what they did wrong. You might think silence avoids conflict, but it actually creates more of it.

Ghosting can feel like safety to you, but it feels like punishment to the other person.

When you are the chaser: You might be the one always reaching out first. You send the text, make the call, plan the hangout, or ask what went wrong. You want connection, not control. But when the other person keeps pulling away, you start to panic.

You might start over-explaining, apologizing too much, or begging for clarity. You might even blame yourself for their distance. Chasing feels like effort, but it is really fear trying to keep love from leaving.

When this dynamic is unhealthy: Both people are stuck in a loop that feeds itself. The ghost pulls away to feel safe. The chaser moves closer to feel safe. Each person's coping style triggers the other's. The ghost feels smothered. The chaser feels abandoned. No one wins.

The relationship starts to revolve around the chase instead of the connection. The more it happens, the harder it becomes to talk honestly.

When it is healthy: Healthy space does not cause fear. Healthy closeness does not cause pressure. Both people can say what they need and trust that the relationship will survive distance.

The ghost learns to speak instead of disappear. The chaser learns to pause instead of panic. Each person starts to trust that love can exist even in silence.

How to make it healthier: If you tend to ghost, learn to communicate your need for space before you take it. Say, "I care about you, but I need some time to clear my head. I'll reach out when I'm ready." This keeps trust alive even during distance.

If you tend to chase, try to sit with the discomfort of not knowing. Take a breath instead of sending another message. Remind yourself that someone's silence does not automatically mean rejection. Focus your energy on calm, not control.

If both of you recognize this pattern, talk about it during a peaceful moment. The ghost can say, "When I pull away, it is not because I don't care. I just get overwhelmed." The chaser can say, "When you disappear, I start to feel anxious and unsure. It helps when you tell me you'll come back."

Once both people understand what the other is afraid of, the whole pattern begins to change.

Healthy relationships have both space and closeness. They breathe. When the ghost feels safe enough to stay and the chaser feels safe enough to rest, love stops running and finally gets to stand still.

The Pleaser–Controller Dynamic

The pleaser–controller dynamic forms when one person works hard to keep the peace, and the other works hard to stay in control. The pleaser avoids conflict at all costs. The controller needs things done a certain way to feel safe. Together, they create a relationship that looks calm from the outside but feels tense underneath.

It can happen in any relationship. One person gives in, the other directs. It may seem like things "work," but deep down, both people are walking on eggshells.

When you are the pleaser: You care deeply about keeping everyone happy. You say yes when you want to say no. You smooth things over, apologize first, and take the blame just to make things calm again. You might tell yourself you are being kind, but most of the time, you are being scared.

You fear that conflict means rejection. So instead of speaking up, you go along with what others want. It feels easier in the moment, but it slowly builds quiet resentment. You begin to disappear inside your own relationships.

When you are the controller: You like things a certain way. You want to feel steady and secure. When people disagree or make mistakes, it makes you uncomfortable. So you try to manage them, plan ahead, or take over.

You may not mean to be controlling. To you, it feels like leadership. But over time, it starts to feel like pressure to the other person. You may notice that people around you withdraw, shut down, or stop offering opinions.

When you see that happening, it is a sign that control has started replacing trust.

When this dynamic is unhealthy: The pleaser loses their voice. The controller loses their softness. Both people lose connection.

The pleaser begins to feel trapped. The controller begins to feel alone. The relationship turns into a performance where one person manages and the other quietly obeys.

There is peace on the surface but tension underneath. It is the kind of calm that feels like holding your breath.

When it is healthy: In a healthy version of this dynamic, the pleaser learns that honesty builds stronger peace than avoidance. The controller learns that trust builds stronger safety than control. Both people start meeting in the middle — one speaks up, the other listens.

Healthy relationships are not free of conflict. They are full of safety. You can disagree and still feel connected.

How to make it healthier: If you are the pleaser, practice using your voice even when it shakes. Start small. Say, "Actually, I'd rather not," or "That doesn't work for me." You do not have to argue. You just have to be honest. Each time you do, you remind yourself that love can handle truth.

If you are the controller, practice letting go of small things. Let someone else decide the plan or make a choice that feels different from yours. When you feel the need to correct, pause and ask, "Is this about safety or control?"

If both of you see this pattern, talk about it. The pleaser can say, "I hide my feelings to avoid conflict, but it's making me tired." The controller can say, "I take over because I worry things will fall apart. I don't want to keep doing that."

Once both sides are spoken out loud, real peace begins to grow.

You do not have to be perfect to be loved, and you do not have to be in control to be safe. You just have to be honest and present.

That is how the pleaser and the controller learn to become partners instead of opposites.

The Peacemaker–Firestarter Dynamic

The peacemaker-firestarter dynamic happens when one person avoids conflict and the other creates it to feel heard or in control. One values calm. The other values intensity. Together, they create a cycle of quiet and chaos that repeats over and over.

This pattern can show up anywhere — in friendships, families, or romantic relationships. It starts because both people are trying to meet the same need in opposite ways. The peacemaker wants safety. The firestarter wants connection. But both end up feeling misunderstood.

When you are the peacemaker: You work hard to keep things smooth. You avoid arguments. You hold back your opinions because you do not want to make things worse. When tension builds, you go quiet or walk away. You think that silence will calm things down, but it often makes the other person feel ignored.

You tell yourself that you are protecting the relationship by staying calm. In reality, you are hiding from the discomfort that could lead to real understanding.

When you are the firestarter: You are not trying to start fights for fun. You start them because you want to feel seen. You raise your voice, ask questions, or push buttons because silence feels unbearable. Even though you know it will create tension, you would rather argue than feel invisible.

You may not realize that the harder you push, the more the peacemaker pulls away. The louder you get, the quieter they become. You both end up proving your own fear true. You feel ignored. They feel attacked.

When this dynamic is unhealthy: Both people are trapped in a loop that feeds itself. The peacemaker's silence makes the firestarter louder. The firestarter's anger makes the peacemaker quieter. Each person's way of coping makes the other more afraid.

The peacemaker begins to feel like they are living in a storm. The firestarter begins to feel like they are shouting into a void. Over time, connection fades.

When it is healthy: Healthy communication is not about choosing between quiet and loud. It is about both people learning to express and listen. The peacemaker learns that speaking honestly brings real peace. The firestarter learns that calm listening brings real power.

When the relationship is healthy, both can stay present in uncomfortable moments. They no longer fear each other's feelings. Conflict becomes a bridge, not a wall.

How to make it healthier: If you are the peacemaker, practice staying in the conversation even when it feels uncomfortable. You can stay calm without shutting down. Try saying, "I need a minute to think, but I want to keep talking." That shows you are still here, even if you need space to breathe.

If you are the firestarter, practice using a softer tone and slower pace. You can express passion without aggression. When you feel yourself heating up, take a breath and say, "I want to talk about this, but I want it to come out right." That keeps the door open instead of slamming it shut.

If both of you see this dynamic, name it out loud. The peacemaker can say, "When things get intense, I shut down because I get scared." The firestarter can say, "When you go quiet, I panic because I feel like I don't matter." Once both fears are named, understanding can grow.

Peace is not the absence of conflict. It is the presence of safety. When both people learn to speak and listen with care, the firestarter's passion and the peacemaker's calm can finally work together instead of against each other.

The Judge–Defendant Dynamic

The judge–defendant dynamic happens when one person takes the role of critic and the other takes the role of defense. One points out what is wrong. The other spends their energy trying to explain or prove their side. This pattern can form in any relationship, but it often hides underneath habits like "giving feedback," "helping someone improve," or "just being honest."

It starts with good intentions. The judge wants to make things better. The defendant wants to keep the peace. But over time, it stops feeling like teamwork and starts feeling like trial.

When you are the judge: You might notice small details that others miss. You care about doing things right. You want to help, to correct, or to make sure people see what you see. You probably tell yourself that you are being helpful or truthful. But sometimes, your truth starts to sound like judgment.

You might notice people around you shutting down, avoiding feedback, or getting defensive. When that happens, it is not because they don't want to grow. It is because they do not feel safe.

When you are the defendant: You may feel like you can never get it right. You try to explain, justify, or calm things down, but it never feels like enough. You might replay conversations in your head, wondering how you could have said things differently.

You tell yourself that you are being careful, but really, you are being small. You shrink to avoid being criticized. You focus more on being right than being real.

When this dynamic is unhealthy: The relationship starts to lose warmth. The judge becomes the authority. The defendant becomes the student. Conversations feel tense. One person speaks to correct. The other speaks to defend. Nobody feels understood.

The judge may grow frustrated that no one listens. The defendant may grow tired of feeling scolded. Both people end up alone inside their roles.

When it is healthy: Healthy relationships have accountability without shame. The judge learns that truth lands best when it is spoken with kindness. The defendant learns that feedback is not always rejection. Both people learn to talk in ways that build trust instead of fear.

In healthy connection, correction becomes collaboration. The goal shifts from "who is right" to "how can we make this work."

How to make it healthier: If you tend to be the judge, pause before offering feedback. Ask yourself, "Am I saying this to help or to control?" Then check your tone. Sometimes it is not what you say, but how you say it.

Try adding grace to your honesty. Instead of "You always mess this up," say, "This part could be stronger. Want to work on it together?" It is the same truth, but it lands differently.

If you tend to be the defendant, practice listening without explaining. You can hear someone's point without agreeing with it. Try saying, "I hear what you mean," instead of rushing to justify. It will calm the tone of the whole conversation.

If both people see this pattern, talk about it when things are calm. The judge can say, "I don't want to come across as harsh. I'm trying to help, but I know my tone matters." The defendant can say, "I get defensive because I want you to see that I care. I'm not trying to fight."

Once both sides understand that they are reacting from care, not cruelty, the relationship softens.

Growth happens when truth and grace can share the same space. When honesty feels safe, no one has to play the judge or the defendant anymore.

The Caretaker–Avoider Dynamic

The caretaker-avoider dynamic forms when one person gives too much and the other pulls away. The caretaker wants closeness. The avoider wants space. At first, this can feel balanced. One person likes to care. The other likes to be independent. But over time, the gap between giving and receiving becomes too wide.

The caretaker starts to feel unseen. The avoider starts to feel smothered. Neither one is wrong, but both are trapped in a pattern that quietly drains connection.

When you are the caretaker: You lead with kindness. You check in, ask questions, and make sure everyone else is okay. You remember birthdays, bring coffee, or handle details that others forget. You take pride in being dependable.

But sometimes, caring becomes control. You give even when no one asked. You take responsibility for someone else's feelings. You believe that if you just love harder, the other person will finally relax, open up, or change.

You might tell yourself that you're being selfless, but often, you're hoping your effort will make you feel secure.

When you are the avoider: You value space and independence. You need time alone to think or reset. When someone cares too much or gets too close, it can feel overwhelming. You may pull away, not because you don't care, but because closeness feels like pressure.

You might not say what you feel because you fear disappointing people. Instead, you disappear, stay quiet, or focus on something else. To the caretaker, this looks cold. To you, it feels safe.

When this dynamic is unhealthy: The caretaker keeps reaching out, hoping for connection. The avoider keeps pulling away, hoping for peace. Each person's way of coping fuels the other's fear. The caretaker feels rejected. The avoider feels trapped.

Eventually, both people get tired. The caretaker starts to feel resentful. The avoider starts to feel guilty. Love turns into tension.

When it is healthy: Healthy relationships have both care and space. The caretaker learns that love does not require constant doing. The avoider learns that closeness does not erase freedom. Both people start trusting that connection can exist even without constant effort.

When this dynamic is balanced, the caretaker still gives, but with boundaries. The avoider still takes space, but with communication. Both learn to respect what the other needs.

How to make it healthier: If you are the caretaker, check your motives before helping. Ask, "Am I doing this because they need it, or because I need to feel needed?" Give space without withdrawing love. Let others come to you sometimes.

If you are the avoider, practice staying present even when it feels uncomfortable. You can ask for space without disappearing. Say, "I care about you, but I need some time to recharge." That honesty keeps trust alive.

If both of you notice this pattern, talk about it when things are calm. The caretaker can say, "I know I can be too helpful when I feel distance." The avoider can say, "I know I shut down when I feel pressure." Once those truths are spoken, both sides soften.

Love needs both oxygen and warmth. Too much care smothers. Too much distance freezes. When both people learn to balance effort and space, the relationship breathes again.

The caretaker learns that love is stronger when it is calm. The avoider learns that peace is easier when they stay connected. Together, they learn that real love is not about chasing or escaping. It is about learning how to stay.

The Anchor–Drifter Dynamic

The anchor–drifter dynamic happens when one person stays steady while the other moves in and out. The anchor values consistency and routine. The drifter values freedom and change. At first, this can feel balanced. The anchor provides security. The drifter brings energy and adventure. But if the balance tips too far, both end up feeling frustrated and alone.

This dynamic can show up in any relationship. One person holds things together. The other moves with the wind. The anchor feels like they are waiting. The drifter feels like they are being held down.

When you are the anchor: You take pride in being dependable. You show up when you say you will. You keep things organized and make plans for the future. You are the one who follows through, checks in, and makes sure everyone is okay.

But sometimes, that steadiness can start to feel like control. You might try to keep people close when they need space. You might feel hurt or anxious when they pull away. You want stability so badly that you hold tighter instead of trusting that people will return.

When you are the drifter: You like movement. You change jobs, hobbies, or plans easily. You get excited about new ideas and experiences. You are not trying to run from people, but you feel most alive when you have room to explore.

You may not notice how your freedom affects those who care about you. When you disappear for a while, the anchor feels forgotten. When you return, you may find that they are guarded or distant. You think they should be happy to see you, but they are still hurting from when you left.

When this dynamic is unhealthy: The anchor begins to feel lonely and used. They stop trusting that the drifter will stay. The drifter begins to feel trapped and misunderstood. They stop communicating because every conversation feels like guilt or pressure.

The anchor becomes heavier. The drifter floats farther away. Eventually, both feel disconnected.

When it is healthy: Healthy relationships have both steadiness and flow. The anchor learns to trust movement. The drifter learns to respect commitment. Together, they create a rhythm that has both roots and wings.

When this dynamic is balanced, the anchor can say, "I trust you'll come back," and the drifter can say, "I'll make sure you know where I am." The relationship feels flexible, not fragile.

How to make it healthier: If you are the anchor, loosen your grip without giving up your boundaries. Remember that love is not proven by proximity. It is proven by consistency over time. Trust that space does not mean abandonment. Focus on your own life when the drifter pulls away. The more grounded you are, the less you'll fear distance.

If you are the drifter, communicate before you move. Say, "I need some time to do my own thing, but I'll check in on this day." A few words can turn what looks like avoidance into reassurance. If you want people to trust you, show them reliability even in your freedom.

If both of you see this pattern, talk about what safety looks like for each of you. The anchor might say, "I feel secure when I know what to expect." The drifter might say, "I feel loved when I'm trusted to be myself." Both can honor those needs without judgment.

When the anchor stops holding too tightly and the drifter stops running too far, the relationship finally finds balance. Stability and freedom can exist together.

The truth is, the world needs both anchors and drifters. Anchors remind us where home is. Drifters remind us that home can move with us. When both remember they are on the same ocean, the connection stops feeling like a tug of war and starts feeling like a tide.

The Critic–Performer Dynamic

The critic–performer dynamic happens when one person takes the role of evaluator and the other takes the role of achiever. The critic measures, comments, and corrects. The performer tries to meet those standards to earn approval or peace.

It can show up in any type of relationship — between partners, parents and children, friends, or even coworkers. At first, it may look productive. The critic wants things done well. The performer wants to please. But over time, both end up feeling empty.

When you are the critic: You notice details that others miss. You care about quality and high standards. You may not think of yourself as critical, only honest. You believe that feedback helps people grow.

But sometimes, your feedback starts sounding like judgment. You might sigh, correct, or roll your eyes without realizing it. You may think you are helping, but what the other person hears is that they are not enough.

You often carry pressure from your own past. Maybe someone once held you to impossible standards, so now you hold others the same way. What felt like survival for you may now feel like rejection for them.

When you are the performer: You try hard to impress. You watch for small signs of approval — a smile, a kind word, or even just silence. You might stay busy or perfect every detail just to avoid hearing that you did something wrong.

At first, it feels rewarding. When the critic is pleased, you feel safe. But when they are disappointed, it cuts deep. You begin to connect your worth to how well you perform. Eventually, you may lose sight of who you are outside of the applause.

When this dynamic is unhealthy: The critic feels responsible for holding standards. The performer feels responsible for maintaining peace. Both live in quiet tension. The critic believes, "If I don't say something, they'll never improve." The performer believes, "If I mess up, they'll stop loving me."

Conversations become checklists instead of connection. Mistakes feel dangerous. The relationship loses warmth.

When it is healthy: Healthy accountability is kind and balanced. The critic learns to guide without shaming. The performer learns to receive feedback without letting it define them. Both people understand that love and approval are not the same thing.

In a healthy version of this dynamic, encouragement replaces evaluation. You can still have high standards, but they come from care, not fear. The performer starts to feel safe enough to relax, and the critic begins to see that gentleness does more good than pressure.

How to make it healthier: If you are the critic, soften your delivery. Speak encouragement before correction. Say, "I appreciate how much effort you put into this," before you offer your feedback. It reminds the other person that you see their heart, not just their flaws.

If you are the performer, practice separating your value from your performance. When someone gives feedback, listen, but do not turn it into a verdict about who you are. Remind yourself, "This is about what I did, not who I am."

If both of you see this pattern, talk about it honestly. The critic can say, "I give feedback because I care, but I see how it can sound harsh." The performer can say, "I know I take things personally, but I want to learn how to handle it better."

Honesty without attack heals this pattern.

The critic learns that people grow best when they feel safe. The performer learns that approval is nice, but authenticity is better. When both let go of fear, the relationship shifts from performance to partnership.

Real love does not need an audience or a review. It grows when people can show up imperfectly and still feel accepted.

The Savior–Martyr Dynamic

The savior-martyr dynamic happens when two people bond through sacrifice. One steps in to rescue, and the other proves their worth by suffering. It can look noble, loyal, and loving, but underneath, both people are trying to earn love instead of simply receiving it.

At first, it feels meaningful. The savior feels important. The martyr feels valued. Both get something out of the struggle. But the longer it continues, the heavier it gets. One feels drained. The other feels trapped.

When you are the savior: You want to help. You want to fix things. You see someone hurting and feel responsible for making it right. You step in quickly, sometimes before you are even asked. It makes you feel strong, needed, and caring.

But over time, helping turns into carrying. You start to take on pain that is not yours. You may grow resentful that others do not do as much for you as you do for them. You may even start to believe that if you stop helping, everything will fall apart.

You give until you are empty, but you still feel like it is not enough.

When you are the martyr: You give too, but in a different way. You prove your loyalty through suffering. You might stay in hard situations because you believe that love means endurance. You tell yourself that pain shows how much you care.

You might not ask for help because you do not want to be a burden. You might say yes when you mean no. Deep down, you are hoping someone will finally see how much you have done and come to your rescue.

When this dynamic is unhealthy: The savior feels unappreciated. The martyr feels unseen. The savior begins to see themselves as the only strong one. The martyr begins to see themselves as the only selfless one. Both feel misunderstood and exhausted.

Conversations often circle around guilt and obligation. The relationship becomes a loop of giving, resenting, apologizing, and then giving again.

When it is healthy: Healthy love does not require either person to lose themselves. The savior learns that helping without boundaries is not kindness. The martyr learns that love does not need suffering to prove itself. Both start to find value in being, not just in doing.

When this dynamic is balanced, both can offer and receive without guilt. There is mutual respect instead of silent sacrifice.

How to make it healthier: If you are the savior, pause before jumping in. Ask, "Do they need my help, or am I helping to feel needed?" Offer support that empowers instead of replaces. Let others handle their own growth. You can care deeply without carrying their weight.

If you are the martyr, learn to ask for help and set boundaries. Stop defining love by how much pain you can handle. Practice saying, "I can't do that right now," or "I need rest." That is not weakness. It is wisdom.

If both of you notice this pattern, talk about it openly. The savior can say, "I realize I take on too much because I want to feel useful." The martyr can say, "I let things hurt too long because I think it makes me loyal." Naming the truth breaks the pattern.

Love grows stronger when it is shared, not sacrificed. Real strength is not found in rescuing or suffering. It is found in balance, where both people give from a full heart and rest when they need to.

The savior learns that the world does not fall apart when they let go. The martyr learns that love does not disappear when they stand up. Together, they learn that connection does not need saving. It needs honesty and rest.

The Child–Child Dynamic

The child–child dynamic happens when two people in a relationship both avoid responsibility. Neither wants to lead or make hard decisions. Both prefer comfort over accountability. It can feel fun and light at first, but eventually, someone has to grow up or everything falls apart.

This dynamic is common in friendships, romantic relationships, and even work partnerships. It starts because both people want to escape pressure. They bond over ease. They say things like, "Let's not make it a big deal," or "We'll figure it out later." But later rarely comes.

When you are one of the children: You may love adventure, fun, and freedom. You do what feels right in the moment and avoid anything that feels heavy. You may avoid conflict, planning, or structure. You tell yourself that you are "going with the flow," but deep down, you might just be avoiding responsibility.

When things get hard, you may joke it off or change the subject. You want to feel good, not serious. But when two people live like this together, important things start slipping through the cracks. Bills, plans, promises, even emotional needs get ignored.

When this dynamic is unhealthy: The relationship becomes unstable. There is no one steering the ship. Small problems turn into big ones because no one steps up to deal with them.

At first, it may feel like freedom, but after a while, it feels like chaos. One person usually starts to get tired first. They might quietly start taking on more responsibility, which then changes the dynamic into something else entirely, like parent–child. The laughter starts to fade, replaced by frustration and disappointment.

Both people may begin to feel stuck, waiting for the other to grow up first.

When it is healthy: Healthy relationships have room for play, but also for responsibility. The child–child dynamic can still work if both people learn balance. You can keep the fun and lightness while still showing up for real life.

In a healthy version, both people learn to be dependable without losing their joy. You still laugh together, but you also follow through. You still dream big, but you also take action. You can be free and still be accountable.

How to make it healthier: If you notice this pattern, start small. Take ownership of one thing at a time. Keep a promise. Follow through on a plan. Show up when you said you would. You do not have to lose your spontaneity. You just need to prove that you can be trusted.

If both people see this happening, talk about what responsibility means for each of you. You can say, "I love how fun we are, but I want us to also be reliable." That helps shift the tone without killing the connection.

Sometimes, the fear of growing up comes from old wounds. You might associate responsibility with pressure or failure. But maturity does not mean losing your spark. It means learning how to protect it.

When both people start showing up as adults who still know how to play, everything changes. Trust grows. Fun feels real again because it is built on a foundation that lasts.

You do not have to pick between joy and responsibility. The best relationships have both.

When two people decide to keep the laughter but add accountability, the child–child dynamic becomes something powerful. It becomes a relationship where both people feel free, safe, and seen — not because they are escaping life, but because they are finally living it.

The Anchor–Storm Dynamic

The anchor-storm dynamic happens when one person stays calm and steady while the other moves through strong emotions and reactions. The anchor values stability. The storm values expression. Together, they create a rhythm that can either balance or break the relationship.

At first, the match can feel beautiful. The anchor admires the storm's passion and fire. The storm feels safe in the anchor's steadiness. But over time, those same qualities can start to clash. The anchor begins to feel drained. The storm begins to feel misunderstood.

When you are the anchor: You keep things grounded. You are the one who stays calm when emotions run high. You do not like chaos or unpredictability. When someone gets loud or upset, you pull back or shut down. You may believe that calm means control.

You think you are protecting the peace, but sometimes, your calm can feel like distance. When the storm is raging, silence can sound like not caring. You may not mean to withdraw, but your quiet feels like rejection to someone who needs to feel heard.

When you are the storm: You feel things deeply. You express what others keep hidden. When something feels wrong, you say it. When you love, you love hard. You bring energy, honesty, and emotion into everything.

But sometimes, your intensity can be overwhelming. You speak before thinking. You raise your voice. You move fast and expect others to keep up. You may not realize that your passion can sound like pressure to the people around you.

You want connection, not control, but your energy can make others retreat.

When this dynamic is unhealthy: The more the storm feels ignored, the louder they become. The more the anchor feels overwhelmed, the quieter they become. Each person's way of coping triggers the other's.

The storm starts to believe the anchor does not care. The anchor starts to believe the storm will never calm down. The relationship becomes a loop of shouting and silence.

Eventually, both people feel unseen. The anchor feels unappreciated for holding things together. The storm feels unloved for showing emotion.

When it is healthy: Healthy balance happens when both people learn from each other. The anchor learns that calm does not mean silence. The storm learns that expression does not mean explosion.

When this dynamic is healthy, emotions are allowed, but they do not control everything. The anchor stays grounded while still engaging. The storm feels free to express without losing respect. Together, they create safety and movement at the same time.

How to make it healthier: If you are the anchor, stay steady but present. Do not disappear into quiet. When the storm is emotional, say, "I hear you, and I want to understand, but I need a moment to process." That shows care without losing balance.

If you are the storm, slow down when your emotions rise. Take a breath before you speak. Remind yourself that intensity does not always equal truth. Say, "I need to talk about this, but I want to do it calmly."

If both of you see this pattern, talk about it when things are peaceful. The anchor can say, "Sometimes I shut down when things get intense, but I want to stay connected." The storm can say, "Sometimes I push too hard because I'm scared of being ignored." That honesty helps both sides feel safe.

When the anchor and the storm learn to trust each other's nature, their differences stop being a problem and start being a gift. The storm teaches the anchor how to feel. The anchor teaches the storm how to breathe.

Together, they build a relationship that can handle anything — not by avoiding emotion, but by learning how to stand in it without breaking.

The Performer–Audience Dynamic

The performer–audience dynamic happens when one person feels responsible for entertaining, impressing, or keeping things exciting, while the other mainly observes or reacts. One performs. The other watches. It can look lighthearted and fun at first, but over time, it can become lonely for both people.

This pattern often begins with admiration. The performer loves to be seen. The audience loves to watch. The connection feels easy because both get what they need. The performer feels valued. The audience feels inspired. But when the show never ends, real connection never begins.

When you are the performer: You bring energy and personality wherever you go. You make people laugh. You tell good stories. You know how to make others feel entertained and comfortable. You take pride in that, and it often comes from a kind heart.

But sometimes, performing becomes protection. You use humor or charm to avoid vulnerability. You may fill silences with words or jokes because quiet feels risky. You might think, "If I keep everyone happy, no one will leave."

You are not trying to fake it. You are trying to feel safe. But constant performance can become exhausting, and eventually, you may wonder if people like you for who you are or just for the show you put on.

When you are the audience: You enjoy the performer's energy. You admire their confidence and their ability to keep things light. It is easy to let them lead every moment. You might think, "They love being the center of attention," so you step back and let them.

But over time, your silence can start to feel like distance. The performer begins to feel alone, like they have to carry the relationship. You might not mean to, but by staying quiet, you accidentally create space between you.

When this dynamic is unhealthy: The performer starts to feel unseen behind the act. The audience starts to feel disconnected, unsure how to join in. Every conversation feels like a stage. There is energy but not intimacy.

The performer grows tired of entertaining. The audience grows tired of watching. Both begin to crave something real, but neither knows how to ask for it.

When it is healthy: Healthy connection means both people take turns being seen and heard. The performer can still bring energy, but also honesty. The audience can still enjoy the moment, but also participate. When both share the stage, the relationship feels balanced and alive.

In a healthy version, laughter and depth exist side by side. The performer can be real without fear, and the audience can engage without hesitation.

How to make it healthier: If you are the performer, try leaving space for silence. Let someone else speak first. When you feel the urge to fill the room, pause instead. Say, "Tell me about you," and really listen. You might be surprised how good it feels to not have to perform.

If you are the audience, step forward. Ask questions. Share your thoughts, even if they are small. Say, "I want to know what you think about this," or "Can I tell you something that's been on my mind?" Participation creates connection.

If both of you notice this pattern, talk about it. The performer can say, "I know I take up a lot of space when I'm nervous. I want to work on that." The audience can say, "Sometimes I stay quiet because I don't want to interrupt you, but I want to be part of the conversation."

When both people feel safe to be seen and to see, the performance ends and the relationship begins.

Love grows in the space where no one is trying to impress anyone. That is where honesty replaces applause and connection replaces control.

The Teacher–Student Dynamic

The teacher–student dynamic happens when one person naturally takes on the role of guide and the other becomes the learner. At first, this feels supportive. The teacher enjoys sharing wisdom. The student feels safe being led. But over time, the balance can shift. One person becomes the authority. The other becomes dependent. What started as growth can slowly turn into control.

This pattern often begins with good intentions. The teacher truly wants to help. The student truly wants to improve. Both care about each other, but the relationship begins to revolve around lessons instead of connection.

When you are the teacher: You like to help people see things clearly. You explain, advise, and share what you know. It feels natural to step into the leadership role. You may think you are helping someone "reach their potential," and sometimes, you really are.

But teaching can quietly turn into preaching. You might stop listening and start instructing. You may find yourself giving advice even when it is not asked for. It starts to feel like your value comes from being right instead of being present.

You mean well, but over time, your lessons can make the other person feel small instead of supported.

When you are the student: You admire the teacher. You trust their opinion. You ask for help often because you believe they know better. It feels good to have someone who seems to have the answers.

But over time, you may stop trusting your own judgment. You might wait for approval before making decisions. You might start thinking that disagreeing is disrespectful. You begin to shrink your own voice so the teacher can keep theirs.

When this dynamic is unhealthy: The teacher begins to feel powerful but also pressured to always have the answers. The student begins to feel dependent and quietly frustrated. The relationship becomes uneven. One leads, the other follows, but neither grows.

Eventually, the teacher may feel unappreciated. The student may feel unseen. Both get stuck in roles they no longer want.

When it is healthy: Healthy guidance is a two-way exchange. The teacher stays humble enough to keep learning. The student stays confident enough to think for themselves. Both share ideas, and both listen.

When this dynamic is balanced, the teacher says, "What do you think?" as often as they say, "Here's what I think." The student feels encouraged to explore instead of imitate.

The best teaching happens when both people grow together.

How to make it healthier: If you are the teacher, step back sometimes. Let silence teach. Resist the urge to always fix or explain. Say, "I trust you to figure this out," and mean it. When you let people find their own answers, your guidance becomes a gift, not a leash.

If you are the student, start trusting your own instincts. Before asking for advice, pause and ask yourself, "What do I think?" You may realize you already know the answer. Share your opinion even if it feels uncertain. Growth happens through trying, not just learning.

If both of you see this pattern, talk about it kindly. The teacher can say, "I know I can be too quick to guide, but I trust your wisdom." The student can say, "I appreciate your help, but I want to learn to trust myself more."

When both sides are honest, the relationship deepens. The teacher learns to listen. The student learns to speak. The connection shifts from hierarchy to partnership.

In the end, the best teachers are those who make themselves unnecessary. The best students are those who learn to stand beside their teachers, not beneath them. That is where respect turns into friendship, and learning turns into love.

The Pleaser–Judge Dynamic

The pleaser–judge dynamic happens when one person tries to earn approval while the other becomes the one who gives or withholds it. The pleaser works hard to keep the relationship peaceful. The judge measures, corrects, or evaluates. One wants harmony. The other wants control.

This pattern can begin quietly. The pleaser starts adapting to the judge's moods. The judge starts expecting that. Over time, the pleaser loses their voice, and the judge loses their compassion. Both end up lonely, even though they are still together.

When you are the pleaser: You do whatever it takes to keep things smooth. You agree even when you disagree. You avoid conflict because you want peace. You want to be liked, respected, and accepted. You tell yourself that keeping everyone happy means keeping the relationship safe.

But it does not stay safe. Each time you hide your opinion or ignore your feelings, you disappear a little more. You stop being known. You become whatever you think someone else needs you to be. You may not notice how tired that makes you until one day, you realize you feel invisible.

When you are the judge: You believe that your standards keep things together. You notice what others could do better. You expect effort and discipline. You see correction as caring, because you want to help people grow.

But when you correct more than you connect, people start to fear you instead of trust you. You may not mean to be harsh, but your presence starts to feel heavy. Others start adjusting themselves around you, hoping not to disappoint.

When people stop being honest with you, that is not respect. That is fear dressed up as agreement.

When this dynamic is unhealthy: The pleaser gives up their truth to keep the peace. The judge gives up warmth to keep control. The relationship becomes quiet on the surface but full of unspoken tension. The pleaser feels small. The judge feels misunderstood.

The more the pleaser hides, the more the judge criticizes. The more the judge criticizes, the more the pleaser hides. It is a circle that never ends.

When it is healthy: Healthy connection has both honesty and care. The pleaser learns that saying no does not break love. The judge learns that gentleness does not weaken authority. Both learn that relationships work best when no one has to shrink.

In a healthy version of this dynamic, the pleaser speaks up calmly and confidently. The judge listens without taking it as rebellion. Respect becomes mutual instead of one-sided.

How to make it healthier: If you are the pleaser, start practicing small truths. Say, "I see it differently," or "That doesn't feel right to me." You can be kind and still have a boundary. Remember that being liked is not the same as being loved.

If you are the judge, pause before correcting. Ask, "Is this helpful or just controlling?" Practice appreciation more than evaluation. Tell people what they did right before you talk about what they missed.

If both of you recognize this pattern, talk about it when things are calm. The pleaser can say, "I want to be honest with you, but I get scared when I feel judged." The judge can say, "I hold high standards because I care, but I know it can come off as harsh."

When you both understand what fear sits underneath your behavior, it gets easier to show compassion instead of control.

The pleaser learns to speak the truth without apology. The judge learns to listen without punishment. That is when love begins to feel safe for both.

Real peace is not built on perfection. It is built on honesty, kindness, and the courage to be real.

The Competitor–Competitor Dynamic

The competitor–competitor dynamic happens when both people in a relationship constantly measure themselves against each other. Each wants to do a little better, win a little more, or be the one who comes out on top. It can start as friendly motivation but slowly turns into tension.

This pattern can form between friends, partners, coworkers, or even family. At first, it feels exciting. You push each other. You admire each other's drive. But over time, it stops feeling like teamwork and starts feeling like a silent battle.

When you are one of the competitors: You notice what the other person does well, and instead of feeling proud, you feel pressure. You might think, "I have to do better than that." You start keeping score without meaning to. When they succeed, you feel a sting. When they struggle, you feel relief, then guilt for feeling it.

You are not trying to tear them down. You just want to prove you matter. You may have learned early in life that being the best was the only way to be loved or respected. Now you chase that same feeling in your relationships.

Sometimes, you even hide your struggles because you do not want to look weak. But that makes the distance worse.

When this dynamic is unhealthy: Every win becomes proof of who is ahead. Every loss becomes proof of who is behind. You stop celebrating each other and start comparing. You might downplay their success or exaggerate your own.

The connection starts to feel unsafe. You cannot relax because everything feels like a test. Both of you stop sharing honestly. The friendship or partnership becomes about performance instead of trust.

Eventually, both people get tired of pretending. One withdraws. The other doubles down. What once felt like motivation now feels like competition you never asked for.

When it is healthy: Healthy competition pushes you to grow without making you feel small. It sounds like, "You did great, and that inspires me," instead of, "Now I have to beat you."

When this dynamic is balanced, both people win together. You cheer for each other and help each other improve. You can share success without fear because the relationship is built on respect, not ranking.

How to make it healthier: If you notice this pattern, start by acknowledging it honestly. Say, "I think we sometimes compete instead of celebrate. I don't want it to be that way." That one sentence can take the edge out of the tension.

If you are often the one competing, practice giving compliments without comparison. Say, "That was awesome," and stop there. Do not turn it into, "I need to get to that level too." You can let someone else's win simply be their win.

If both of you notice it, set shared goals instead of separate ones. Compete with each other in fun ways that build connection instead of division. Try learning something new together, exercising together, or working toward the same outcome. That way, competition becomes collaboration.

When both people stop trying to prove who is better, they can start becoming better together.

Success in relationships is not about being number one. It is about being someone others can count on. Real strength shows up in how well you lift others, not how often you outshine them.

When two competitors learn to turn their energy toward growth instead of rivalry, the bond becomes powerful. You stop keeping score and start building something that actually lasts.

The Stranger–Stranger Dynamic

The stranger–stranger dynamic happens when two people are connected by circumstance but not by emotion. They share space, a title, or a routine, but not real understanding. It can happen in long marriages, family relationships, friendships, or workplaces. You might see each other every day but still feel alone.

At first, this dynamic may not feel like a problem. Life is busy. You tell yourself it is normal to drift apart or to have quiet seasons. But when silence lasts too long, distance becomes the new normal.

When you are one of the strangers: You go through the motions. You talk about tasks, plans, or small things, but not feelings. You may tell yourself everything is fine because there is no fighting. But deep down, something feels missing.

You might remember when it felt easier to talk, easier to laugh, or easier to care. You want to reach out but feel awkward, like you are trying to start over with someone you used to know. You worry it will feel forced or that they won't respond the way you hope.

When this dynamic is unhealthy: The relationship becomes quiet in a heavy way. You stop learning new things about each other. You stop showing emotion. There is peace, but not connection.

Both people might secretly feel rejected, even though neither has done anything wrong. The silence starts to feel safer than trying. It becomes easier to stay polite than to be vulnerable.

Eventually, you live side by side but not together. Conversations are short. Days blend together. What was once closeness now feels like a memory.

When it is healthy: Even in the healthiest relationships, there will be quiet seasons. The difference is intention. Healthy quiet feels restful, not empty. Both people know that silence is temporary and connection will return.

Healthy relationships are built on curiosity. You keep asking questions, keep noticing changes, keep showing up even when it feels awkward. You refuse to let comfort turn into distance.

How to make it healthier: If you feel the distance growing, start with something simple. Ask, "How are you really doing?" Say, "I miss talking like we used to." You do not need a big speech. You just need to reach out.

If both of you notice the same quiet gap, talk about it directly. You can say, "I feel like we have become strangers. I want to change that." Then listen. Give space for honesty. The goal is not to go back in time. The goal is to build new closeness with who you both are now.

If the other person does not respond, stay kind but steady. Keep showing small moments of care. Sometimes people are afraid to re-engage because they do not know how. Your patience can remind them it is safe to try.

When two people decide to stop living as strangers, something beautiful happens. The connection might start small — a shared laugh, a deeper conversation, a look that says, "I still see you." That is how closeness begins again.

Every relationship drifts at times. What matters is choosing to turn toward each other again. When both people do, the silence breaks, and the distance starts to close.

You do not have to rebuild everything overnight. Just start with one honest moment. That is all it takes for two strangers to remember that they were always meant to be known.

The Equal Partnership Dynamic

The equal partnership dynamic is what every healthy relationship grows toward. It is the place where both people feel seen, respected, and responsible for their part. No one leads all the time. No one follows all the time. Each person brings their strengths and gives the other space to do the same.

This kind of relationship does not mean everything is always balanced. It means both people keep trying to bring balance back when life tips one way or the other. There is trust, communication, and effort from both sides. It feels safe to be honest, and it feels good to be yourself.

When you are in an equal partnership: You do not have to prove your worth. You do not have to perform or hide. You can say what you think without fear. You can make mistakes and still feel loved. You give freely because you know it will be met with the same care.

You are not keeping score or trying to win. You are both trying to build something that lasts. Each person carries their share of the work, but no one keeps a tally.

What it looks like day to day: Both people listen as much as they speak. Both take responsibility for how they show up. Arguments are not about who is right but about finding understanding. Support goes both ways. Some days one gives more, and some days the other does. There is no pride in who carried more weight. There is gratitude that it was shared at all.

Both people cheer for each other's growth instead of competing. They celebrate together and face struggles together. The relationship becomes a safe foundation where both can grow, not a cage that holds them back.

When this dynamic weakens: Even strong relationships can slip into imbalance. One person might start doing more of the emotional work. The other might get distracted or distant. The difference in an equal partnership is that both notice and care enough to fix it.

You do not ignore the cracks. You talk about them. You take responsibility without blame. You remind each other that the relationship matters more than being right.

How to build or rebuild this dynamic: Start by practicing honesty and curiosity. Ask, "How can I make this feel more equal?" Then listen without defending yourself. Be open to feedback even when it stings.

If you realize you have been giving less, lean back in. If you realize you have been carrying more, speak up calmly. Equality does not mean everything is split in half. It means effort and care flow both ways.

Small actions matter most. Offer help without being asked. Say thank you often. Admit when you are wrong. Forgive quickly. These simple choices create trust.

If you are rebuilding after imbalance, start with small repairs. Apologize for the weight you dropped. Accept the apology for the weight they dropped. Move forward together, not as judge and jury but as partners learning again.

When this dynamic is healthy: You both feel free and connected at the same time. You can lean on each other without losing yourself. You know that love is not about control or dependency. It is about showing up every day as a team.

The equal partnership dynamic is what happens when two people grow enough to meet in the middle. They have learned from every other pattern that came before — the chasing, the pleasing, the judging, the rescuing, the avoiding. Each of those patterns taught them something about what love is not.

Now, they know what it is.

It is steady. It is honest. It is generous. It is equal.

This is the kind of relationship that does not need to be perfect to be strong. It simply needs two people who choose to keep showing up, side by side, again and again.

www.ingramcontent.com/pod-product-compliance
Lightning Source LLC
Chambersburg PA
CBHW071218090426
42736CB00014B/2887